LYNDON BAINES JOHNSON, *PRESIDENT*

John Devaney

Walker and Company
New York

For my in-house political scientist,
John Matthew Devaney

All photos courtesy the Lyndon Baines Johnson Library and Wide World Photos. Map courtesy Barbara Devaney.

First published in the United States of America in 1986 by the Walker Publishing Company, Inc.

Published simultaneously in Canada by John Wiley & Sons Canada, Limited, Rexdale, Ontario.

Library of Congress Cataloging-in-Publication Data

Devaney, John.
  Lyndon Baines Johnson, president.

  (Presidential biography series)
  Includes index.
  1. Johnson, Lyndon B. (Lyndon Baines), 1908–1973 — Juvenile literature. 2. Presidents — United States — Biography — Juvenile literature. I. Title. II. Series.
E847.D48 1986 973.923'092'4 [B] 85-31751
ISBN 0-8027-6638-2
ISBN 0-8027-6639-0 (lib. bdg.)

Text Design by Irwin Wolf
Book Design by Teresa M. Carboni

Printed in the United States of America

10 9 8 7 6 5 4 3 2

Contents

Acknowledgments

I have many people to thank for the material in this book. For many of the photos, my thanks to Harry Middleton and E. Philip Scott of the Lyndon Baines Johnson Library in Austin. The library is on the campus at the University of Texas and a "must" place to visit for anyone who wants to know more about L.B.J.

For all readers, I recommend Robert Caro's *Lyndon Johnson: The Path to Power* (Alfred A. Knopf). This is the first of a three-volume life of Johnson by a Pulitzer-prize winner. Much of the material in the first half of this book comes from Mr. Caro's genius and hard work.

Other books I highly recommend: *Lyndon: An Oral Biography,* by Merle Miller (G.P. Putnam's Sons); *Lyndon B. Johnson, The Exercise of Power,* by Rowland Evans and Robert Novak (New American Library); *The Vantage Point,* by Lyndon Johnson (Holt, Rinehart and Winston).

For teenagers who want to know what life is like for a young person inside the White House, read George Sullivan's *Lynda and Luci Johnson* (Popular Library).

My special thanks to Jeanne Gardner, who should know how important she was.

This map of Texas shows the Hill Country (shaded area) and some of the cities and towns that were the background of Lyndon Johnson's life. San Antonio and Corpus Christi were part of Congressman Kleberg's district. Lyndon's Tenth Congressional District, which he represented from 1937 to 1948, stretched from San Marcos in the south to near Lampasas in the north, and from Brenham in the east to Fredericksburg in the west. The states of Connecticut and Delaware together would fit into this district.

1

A Death in Dallas

The President's open-topped limousine nosed into Dealey Plaza. Seated side by side in the rear were President John F. Kennedy and his wife, Jackie. Another car trailed a few yards behind. Its code name was Halfback. It was packed with Secret Service agents, the president's bodyguards. Behind Halfback in the long motorcade rolled a third car. The vice president and his wife sat in the back seat, their bodyguard and driver in front.

More than 100,000 men, women, and children packed the sidewalks cheering the president on a hot day in Dallas. The time was almost 12:30, the date November 22, 1963. The crowd's loud roar, as people sighted the waving president and first lady, echoed off the plaza's tall buildings.

A cracking sound cut through the roaring. Secret Service men whirled their heads: a rifle shot or a car's backfire? Rufus Youngblood decided in an instant. He spun in his seat and grabbed the rangy vice president by the shoulders, shoving him downward. "Get down!" Rufus shouted.

In the lead car the president tilted in his seat. Jackie turned to look at him. She saw a puzzled frown cross his face. His right hand flicked toward his neck. Before she could speak, she saw the top of her husband's head explode in a shower of crimson bits. A red shower floated down and drenched her pink suit.

The vice president leaves Parkland Hospital on his way to the waiting Air Force One. A secret service agent (on the left) warily eyes the news photographer who took this photograph, making certain he is not a sniper. In his lapel, Lyndon wears a flower for a day that was supposed to have been festive. Behind him walks Representative Homer Thornberry of Texas, unable to contain his tears at the tragedy.

Rufus Youngblood, still pushing down the vice president, heard a voice crackle over his two-way radio. "Halfback to Lawson. The President's been hit. Get us to a hospital fast!"

The three cars lunged forward as drivers stomped on their gas pedals. Youngblood now blanketed the vice president with his bulky body. "An emergency exists!" he said in a low voice. "When we get to where we're going, you and me are going to move right off and not tie in with other people."

2

The vice president's face was pressed close to the floor. From below, Youngblood heard him say in his Texas drawl, "Okay, partner."

Minutes later the three cars jerked to a stop in front of Parkland Memorial Hospital. Youngblood helped the vice president from the car. Four agents spilled out of Halfback and circled him. They glanced left and right at nearby trees. *Was there an army of snipers out there with rifles aimed at the nation's leaders?* The agents hurried the vice president and his petite wife into the hospital and took them to a small room. Blinds were drawn. In another room, surgeons labored over the milk-white body of a president whose life no hands could save.

At 1:13 P.M. a Secret Service agent, face grim, entered the room where the vice president waited. "The president's dead, sir," the agent said.

The vice president's face showed the shock and sickness he later said he felt. He said he wanted to speak to Mrs. Kennedy. Youngblood shook his head. He did not want the vice president roaming where a killer might lurk.

Minutes later a police car streaked, siren silent, through the streets of Dallas. The car carried Youngblood, the vice president, and his wife toward Love Field. There stood the giant Air Force One, the jetliner that had lofted President Kennedy into Dallas this morning.

The police car stopped at Air Force One. Youngblood and other agents huddled around the vice president and his wife as they ran up the boarding steps.

The vice president stepped into the plane's cabin. In a corner a TV screen flashed. The deep voice of CBS reporter Walter Cronkite was finishing a sentence: " ... Lyndon B. Johnson, now president of the United States."

2

The Johnson Strut

"No, Sam," the new mother said to her husband, "I am not cooking breakfast until this baby is named."

Sam Ealy Johnson stared angrily at Rebekah. Their first child, a boy, had been born in August. Now it was November and they had yet to agree on the baby's name.

"How would you like Clarence?" Sam asked. Sam had always yearned to be a lawyer instead of a farmer. Clarence Martin, a good friend, was a lawyer.

"Not in the leastest," Rebekah said, lying in bed and staring fondly at her first baby.

Sam had two other lawyer friends—Dayton Moses and W. C. Linden. "What do you think of Dayton?" he said.

"That is much better, but still not quite the name for this baby." She thought this baby, with its ivory-white skin and jet-black hair, the most beautiful of babies.

"Would you call him Linden?"

Rebekah thought for several moments. "Yes," she said, "if I may spell it as I please." She told Sam that *L-y-n-d-o-n* looked better than *L-i-n-d-e-n.*

"Spell it as you please," Sam said.

"All right," said the former Rebekah Baines. "He is named Lyndon Baines Johnson"—after Sam's friend and Rebekah's father. Only then did she rise from bed to make breakfast.

4

Regardless of the new baby's name, an aunt insisted that he had "the Bunton strain." Eliza Bunton was Lyndon's grandmother. Eliza's father, Robert Bunton, had raised cattle in Texas after the Civil War. He'd driven his herds north on the Chisholm Trail to sell in Abilene. Riding with her daddy, her skin pale and her dark eyes described as "piercing," was Eliza, as daring a rider as any cowpuncher.

The Buntons rode home to Texas with saddlepacks jingling with gold. Then beef prices dropped. Robert Bunton rented his grazing land to other ranchers. The ranchers drove their cattle north, lost many in storms, and had to sell at low prices. They were dreamers and fools, said Robert Bunton, who was a hard-headed landlord.

One of those cowboy fools was Sam Ealy Johnson. His father had come from the South to Texas in a covered wagon. The father had settled along the Perdinales (pronounced Perd 'n' Alice) River in the Hill Country of central Texas. The Hill Country lay some forty miles west of Austin, the state capital. The wavy grassland of the Hill Country seemed ideal to graze cattle and raise cotton. Sam Ealy and his father had to fight off murderous Indians. They built a small fort near the Perdinales. Houses and shanties cropped up near the fort. By 1900, the Indians were gone, and the fort and houses had become a one-street town that called itself a city—Johnson City.

Sam Ealy Johnson also drove cattle north. On one drive he galloped home with $100,000, a fortune in a time when men worked for a dollar a day. Sam bought a bigger ranch for his herds, and he married the dark-haired Bunton girl, Eliza.

Like Robert Bunton, Sam Johnson saw beef prices drop. But he had to gamble on one last drive. Eliza, the practical Bunton, begged him not to. Sam talked of becoming a millionaire. He borrowed money for cowboys and food and set off for Abilene. Storms wiped out half of his herd. He sold the rest at bottom prices. When he came home, he had to sell his ranch to pay his debts.

Rebekah Baines Johnson: The city girl who loved the beautiful and the uplifting things in life found little of either in the Hill Country "dog run" she went to when she married Lyndon's father.

Sam and Eliza settled down on a 433-acre farm along the Perdinales. They tried to grow cotton. But the Hill Country had lost its lushness. Rain, wind, and floods had scrubbed off and washed away the grassy topsoil of the slopes. Each year Sam Johnson carted fewer bales of cotton to market. In 1877 "the Johnsons arrived back on the Perdinales poor," writes Robert Caro in his biography of Lyndon Johnson, *The Years of Lyndon Johnson: The Path to Power,* "and lived there thirty years during which they grew poorer."

Sam Ealy Johnson and Eliza Bunton Johnson had nine children. Their fifth was their first boy, Sam Ealy, Lyndon Johnson's father. He had "the Bunton strain." He was tall, with thick dark hair, a long nose, piercing eyes. He was too poor to go to college, but he dreamed of becoming a lawyer. A flashy dresser, he boasted that "you can tell a man by his boots and his hat and the horse he rides." He strutted, surprising nobody in Johnson City. "All the

Sam Ealy Johnson at his desk in the Texas House of Representatives: The dreamer and the fighter for the "little guy," he wouldn't "go along to get along." His big ears were a Johnson trademark.

Johnsons strutted," folks said. "Hell, the Johnsons strutted sitting down."

Sam dreaded the brutal drudgery of working on his father's farm. In 1905 he campaigned to be elected to the Texas House of Representatives. At twenty-seven he went to Austin as the youngest member of the House.

In 1907 the young legislator was interviewed by an Austin reporter, Rebekah Baines, the daughter of a former legislator. She was a soft-spoken woman who read poetry, loved to attend plays or listen to operas on the newfangled phonographs. She was fascinated by Sam and his "flashing eyes," she told her diary. They dated. He told her how ideals were important to him—like being honest and making better the lives of the poor farmers in the Hill Country. The ideals of love and trust and all "the high things of life" were just as dear to her. Sam and Rebekah talked of making the world a better place. On August 20, 1907, the two dreamers married.

7

Sam took his bride to live on his parents' farm on the Perdinales. The girl who had been raised in a genteel city life was shocked when she saw her new home. It was called a "dog run" in the Hill Country. The unpainted shack was two small rooms piped together by a narrow hall. Behind the dog run was an outhouse.

Sam had to live in a cheap boardinghouse in Austin whenever the legislature met. He was paid only five dollars a day to cover his travel and living costs. He was always broke and often hungry.

Other legislators were rich and well fed. They took fistfuls of money from banks, railroads, gas and electric companies, who paid them to pass laws that would keep wages and taxes down, and prices up. In Austin, Sam was told that "to get along, go along"—in short, to rise in politics, you have to do what those who have power tell you to do.

Sam wouldn't go along. "The farming people and the working people had no one to look after their interests," one Austin politician said years later. "I remember Sam Johnson as a man who truly wanted to help the people who he felt needed help."

When he came back to the Hill Country, Sam rode a horse thirty or forty miles in a day to visit people and ask how he could get help for them in Austin. He was away the night of August 27, 1908, as a rainstorm lashed the Perdinales into a foaming fury. Rebekah told her father-in-law, Sam Ealy, Sr., that she thought she would give birth to her first child that night.

Sam mounted his horse and forded the boiling river to bring back a midwife. She helped to deliver the boy who, three months later, would be named Lyndon Baines Johnson.

At two, little Lyndon put worried looks on his mother's face. When she turned her back, he wandered away to toddle along the riverbank or vanish into the bushy hills. Workers on the farm stared, astonished, when they saw

Lyndon at eighteen months of age: He had his father's big ears and thin-lipped smile—and a liking for wandering off "to get attention."

Lyndon at about age five: The ears are almost covered by the cowboy hat, but on his face is the quizzical and menacing half smile that he would wear as a congressman, senator, vice president, and president.

the tiny figure sway across a field toward them. Lyndon ran away, a cousin once said, "to get attention."

At four, he demanded that his mother send him to a nearby grade school. Kids had to be at least five to go to the school. His mother, who had taught him how to read, adored him. "From the first time I looked into his eyes," she once said, "none of his accomplishments surprised me." She obediently sent him to the school.

A cousin rode her donkey to school each day with Lyndon riding behind her. "I wanna ride in front! I wanna ride in front!" Lyndon hollered. Soon he was riding in front, lashing the donkey with a stick to make it gallop.

By 1913, when Lyndon was five, Sam was the father of two boys and three girls. Sam gave up his job as a legislator and left his father's farm. He moved to Johnson City, fourteen miles away, and began to buy and sell real estate.

"Real-estatin'," he told people, would make him rich. He sold one ranch for a $12,000 profit, a sum few people in Johnson City earned in four years. The Johnsons lived in a white-shingled house, one of the town's best. During the day Rebekah taught, for no pay, the girls of the town. She read poetry and plays to them. She showed them how to dress, walk, and act like city ladies.

At night laughter burst often and loudly from Sam's house. His children, and neighbors' children, gathered around a table lit by a flickering kerosene lamp. Sam divided the children into two sides. The two sides debated — whether, for example, sorghum was sweeter than sugar.

Lyndon, the oldest, was the best in those debates. His father said Lyndon thought on his feet as fast as he himself had when arguing for a bill on the House floor. Lyndon's mother applauded when Lyndon's side won. Sam Houston, Lyndon's younger brother, once said, "We all knew that Lyndon was my mother's favorite — she never much hid it."

After school, the ten-year-old Lyndon played with boys who were fifteen and sixteen. The older boys stared at the thin, pale Lyndon with awe in their eyes. He said so many smart things to pluck them out of trouble. Once they shot at a deer that was too small to be hunted. The deer got away but a grown-up had seen them shoot, and threatened to tell their parents.

The deer wasn't small, Lyndon said. He described a "five-pointer" that they had shot at, a deer that sounded so real even the boys began to believe him. They escaped being spanked and went on looking to Lyndon when they ran into trouble.

Lyndon's father gave him money to buy things other boys were too poor to buy. He came to baseball games with the team's only baseball. He demanded to be the pitcher. The others scowled. "Lyndon," they said, "you throw like a girl." He was always awkward in sports, long legs and pipelike arms getting twisted into pretzels when he ran or threw. When the boys said he couldn't pitch, Lyndon grabbed his baseball and stalked home. "Everything was competition with Lyndon," one boy later said. "He had to win."

"You had to understand why he always had to be out in front, always had to be first," a cousin once said. "You see, he was a Bunton."

When a three-day-old newspaper came to the town's post office, Lyndon snatched it. He ran to Cecil Maddox's barbershop. He sat on a high chair and read the news to men who couldn't read. When the arguing started about something that Lyndon had read, Lyndon's voice piped out as he argued with the grown-ups.

In 1917 his father decided to go back to his first love — politics. He was a Democrat, as were nearly all elected officials in the South since the Civil War. He was easily reelected. When he went to Austin, he took Lyndon along. The teenager walked the floor of the House next to his father. Lyndon met the men — they were called Populists — who sided with his father in trying to help the farmer and the laborer. One of these Populist Democrats was a stumpy,

11

balding legislator from Bonham, in north Texas. His face bulldog grim, Sam Rayburn stood side by side with Sam Johnson as they argued for Populist bills.

Lyndon watched his father try to sway other legislators to vote with him on bills. The six-foot Sam Johnson stood over the legislator, his face—the nose long, the ears big—only inches from the other man's face. He clutched the man's lapels, seeming to pull the man toward him.

The son looked like the father—tall and skinny, big ears, long nose, eyes "dark and piercing," House members later recalled. "They had the same nervous mannerisms," said one Populist, Wright Patman. "They walked the same way. And Lyndon clutched you like his daddy when he talked to you."

Back home in Johnson City, Lyndon practiced what he had learned from his father in Austin. "If there was an argument, he had to win," a pal once recalled. "If he'd differ with you, he'd hover right over you, up against you, breathing right in your face, arguing. . . . He just wouldn't stop until you gave in."

Lyndon sat by his father's side when he rode down dusty roads in his Ford car to campaign at election time. Sam told him about "lead men." A lead man was the leader in a town, village, or farm area. Get the lead man to speak for you, Sam said, and you got from ten to as many as a hundred votes. But this above all, Sam said: Know who was for you, and who was against you.

"If you can't come into a room," Sam told his son, "and tell right away who is for you and who is against you, you don't belong in politics."

You had to read minds! the enthralled Lyndon realized. Down the roads the Ford bounced, father talking politics, son listening raptly—and thinking, as he once said, "I hope this never ends." But it would—when a father gambled and lost.

3

"I'm Going to Be President!"

Sam would be rich. Lyndon's father stood on the small hill overlooking his parents' farm and told himself that this Hill Country would make him rich.

He would get rich on cotton. In the spring of 1920 the price of cotton had soared from twenty cents a pound to fifty cents a pound. World War I had torn apart Europe. Now English, French, and German men and women needed clothes and other goods made of cotton to replace what had been destroyed.

Sam's parents had died in 1917, and he had paid his life's savings, about $20,000, to his brothers and sisters to buy the farm. Then he borrowed $40,000 from banks. He hired workers and bought the best machinery he could buy. He stared dreamily at newspapers that predicted the price of cotton would soon top sixty cents a pound.

Lyndon watched his forty-two-year-old father haul tons of rich riverbottom soil onto the hard gullies of the farm. But spring rains washed the soil back into the Perdinales. Sam dragged more soil into the gullies—and saw rain suck it back to the river.

Summer's unusual heat blistered the cotton he planted. In Europe, factory workers stood on street corners, pockets

13

empty; their factories had turned out too many goods and now had to shut. The price of cotton plunged from forty cents to eight cents a pound.

Sam was ruined. He sold the farm, getting only $10,000— half of what he had paid two years earlier. The $10,000 paid banks and merchants some of what he owed. But he still owed money. IOU notes stood a foot high on his desk. He could work a lifetime and never tear up the last one.

He went back to Johnson City. His brother loaned him money to get back the clapboard house he had sold. Otherwise, the Johnson family would have slept by the side of a road. Sam's wife and children trailed behind him into the house, their ears red, knowing that everyone in town was staring at them, smirking. Sam's gamble on cotton had failed, just as his father's gamble on cattle had failed. Once Sam had strutted, the proud legislator. Now he walked, face grim, head down to avoid the angry eyes of people who wrote him, *"Please pay."*

Sam went to Austin when the legislature opened. He begged for a state job. But to get along, you had to go along. Sam had not gone along. He had said no to powerful men. Now they said no to him.

His oldest child, a stringy, big-eared fourteen-year-old, went to Austin with him. In 1919 he had stared up at his daddy with awe on his face. Now he stood, sullen and ashamed, at the side of a failure. When his father asked him to run an errand, Lyndon turned as though he had not heard. "There wasn't a very friendly feeling between them at all," one legislator said. "He wouldn't pay much attention to anything his father wanted him to do."

Returning to Johnson City, Sam stayed at home. He lived in his bed for weeks. Once he had sipped whiskey with friends. Now he gulped it alone. When he staggered out of his room, bleary-eyed and bearded, he snarled at his children.

Rebekah had relished "the higher things of life." Sam had hired servants to cook and clean. Now there were no more servants. Dishes piled up in sinks, dirty clothes in tubs. The Johnson children went to neighbors' doors asking for meals.

Sam finally got a job working with laborers to pave roads. Before he went to work, he told his oldest child to do chores. When his father left, Lyndon snapped orders to his brother, Sam Houston, and his three little sisters, Rebekah, Lucie, and Josefa. He made them cart in the wood for the fire. "He was like the foreman, the boss," Sam Houston once said. "Well, to put it another way, he was smarter."

Once he brought home three pals. He said to them, "Let's have a race to see who can pile the biggest stack of wood the quickest."

The boys raced to stack wood. One of the other boys won. Lyndon shook his hand and praised him for his quickness. His mother's eyes twinkled as she admired his slyness.

One day Sam came home to see little Lucie lugging wood on her thin shoulders while fifteen-year-old Lyndon barked orders. Sam whacked Lyndon with a paddle. He had to spank him so often that neighbors half a mile away heard Lyndon's howls and said, "Sam's whipping Lyndon again."

Later Lyndon told a cousin that he always howled at the first smack. "My father," he said with a wink, "goes easy after that."

Lyndon seldom talked about his father. He bragged about his grandfather, the cowpuncher. He made up stories about his ancestors that few boys believed. "He was always bragging and telling big lies," one childhood companion later told a Johnson biographer, Robert Caro.

Lyndon was over six feet tall, awkward and clumsy and as skinny as a pole. He walked with the Johnson strut, arms swinging, chin and chest out. He combed his hair even as he walked, piling a high pompadour in front. He slicked the hair down with grease so it shined. "You'd see him coming," a friend said, "and you'd think he was the world's most important person."

The fifteen-year-old Lyndon was looking for an escape from Johnson City. He ran away from home twice— once to California, later to south Texas. His worried father paid a friend ten dollars, more than the bankrupt Sam could afford, to have Lyndon returned by car from south Texas.

One day other boys jeered at something he said. He shouted above their laughter, "Someday I'm going to be president of the United States!"

They laughed louder. One said, "I wouldn't vote for you."

"I won't need your votes," Lyndon shot back.

To the hand-wringing despair of his mother, who loved to read, Lyndon seldom opened a book unless he had to for school. Books bored him—although he hungrily read newspapers, a habit that would last a lifetime. He was always too busy to read a book. One boy said, "He always seemed to be running, running, running."

In June 1924, he graduated from Johnson City's three-year high school. He was fifteen, the youngest of six boys and girls in his class. The other five were going to college. Lyndon said he wouldn't go. He hated to read books, he told a cousin, and knew he would flunk out of college.

And he didn't want to fail, not like his mother, who had a dirty house, and his father, the debtor and drunkard.

He would be somebody. The dreamer in Lyndon told him that. The Bunton in him asked, But *how?*

He began to date the daughter of the richest man in Johnson City, a grocer. Sam owed the grocer a lot of money. The father told his daughter to stop dating Lyndon — and she did.

Lyndon's father nagged him into taking a job on a road-building gang. The pay was two dollars a day for back-aching work in heat and cold. "There's got to be a better way of making a living than this," he told a friend, panting over a shovel. "I want to find a job where I use my brains instead of my hands."

He ran away to California. He worked for a few months for a cousin who was a lawyer. In the spring of 1926 he came back to Johnson City, broke. Maybe his only chance to be a somebody would be in this tiny one-street town. He would make himself the talk of Johnson City.

Now eighteen, he ran around at night with men in their twenties and thirties, men whom local citizens called "the wild bunch." He raced cars down dark roads, once wrecking his father's car. He swilled illegal "moonshine" whiskey. The bunch even stole dynamite and blew up a tree in front of a school.

Rebekah's mother now lived with the Johnsons. Grandma Baines told her daughter, "Mark my words, that boy is going to end up in the penitentiary."

The Johnson City sheriff was thinking along the same lines. Years later Lyndon said, "I was only a hair's breadth away from going to jail."

"You will never be anything except a day laborer," his father told him, "if you don't go to college."

"No, I won't."

"You don't have enough brains to take a college education," Sam growled. Lyndon glared.

He saw himself as the cock of the walk in Johnson City. After all, hadn't he run away to far-off California?

At eighteen he stood a gangling six feet four inches. He strutted his skinny frame by poking out his chest and swinging his long arms.

One night, at a dance, he waltzed cheek to cheek with the girlfriend of a hulking farmhand. The farmhand challenged him to step outside and fight. He bloodied the face and blackened the eye of Lyndon, who boxed as awkwardly as he pitched a baseball. Lyndon slunk home, body bruised. After that humiliation he knew he would never be the strutting cock of the walk in the eyes of girls and boys in Johnson City. He would always be a day laborer, no matter how often he dreamed of being somebody. He knew he had to get out of Johnson City.

But *how?*

The next morning, a January day in 1927, he told his mother that he would leave within a week for college.

4

"The Way You Get Ahead in the World"

Lyndon stood at the door, head bowed. "Won't you help a poor boy?" he asked.

"No," said the husky college student. Clayton Stribling was from Johnson City and he detested Lyndon because he bragged so much.

"Won't you help a poor boy?" Lyndon asked again.

"How long do you want to stay?"

"Thirty days."

"All right," Clayton muttered. Lyndon said thanks and brought in his cheap suitcase. Now he had a roof over his head—at least for thirty days—here at Southwest Texas State Teachers College in San Marcos (the two-year school was best known as San Marcos). But he was still "one scared chicken," as his cousin, also a freshman, had said earlier that day.

He was a gawky chicken. Lyndon towered like an oil derrick over the other students. His worn jacket ended halfway between a knobby elbow and a bony wrist.

And he had reason to be scared. He came to San Marcos knowing he had no place to stay. He didn't have enough money to pay for a year's rent, food, and tuition—about four hundred dollars. And he knew he would have to pass a test to get into San Marcos.

Now, at least, he wouldn't have to pay rent for thirty days. Stribling's room, over a garage, was given free to the football team's captain. That was Boody Johnson (no relation to Lyndon). Boody shared the room with Stribling, also a football player. The quiet Boody enjoyed Lyndon's loud way and barnyard jokes.

After getting Stribling's approval to stay, Lyndon ran with his long strides to see Cecil Evans, the president of the college. "Prexy," as students called Evans, had met Lyndon's father when Sam argued in the legislature to get money for teachers' colleges. Prexy put Lyndon to work raking leaves. The pay was eight dollars a month. With his savings, Lyndon now could pay for a month's tuition and dinner—the only meal he could afford—at a boardinghouse.

He had to pass the entrance test within two weeks. He hitchhiked the thirty miles to Johnson City, where he studied at the knees of his first teacher, to whom he wrote words like these: "Mother, I love you so much, don't neglect me...."

Rebekah taught him what he had forgotten in the three years he had been out of school, and he passed the test.

Over dinner at the boardinghouse, he said that he had passed because his IQ was 145 (it was much lower). He showed the other students a tie, saying he had bought it in Austin for a dollar (a lot of money for a tie in those days). Another boy said he was a liar. He had seen that tie in a five-and-dime store. Lyndon shrugged. The next evening he was telling another group the same story.

"I can still see Lyndon," one of Johnson's fellow students told Robert Caro years later, "reaching out to gobble food and all the time talking, talking, talking." Another said, "It just seemed like he had to lie about everything." Soon he had a nickname: Bull. The name did not refer to his strength.

He began to chat with Prexy Evans, who seldom talked to anyone, not even professors. Lyndon saw something inside Prexy: a liking to talk politics the way other people liked to talk about baseball players or movie stars. Lyndon began to feed Prexy stories about politicians he had met in Austin.

Prexy, delighted, wanted more. He made Lyndon his office boy. The pay was fifteen dollars a month. Now, by borrowing from banks and relatives, he could pay for his tuition and food. And Clayton had dropped out of school, so Lyndon now lived with Boody rent-free.

Boody was the leader of a campus society called the Black Stars. They had the best parties and dated the prettiest girls. "They were the 'in people,' " Lyndon's cousin, Ava, once said. Lyndon asked Boody to make him a member. The other Black Stars said no. They didn't want Bull Johnson around—he bragged too much.

There were three girls to one boy at the college, so most boys could easily get a date. Lyndon seldom had a date. Girls said they would rather stay at home than go out with Lyndon to hear him brag.

He still frowned when he had to open a book. During the spring term of 1927, his first semester, he got C's and D's. Debating was his best subject. Lyndon bragged to other students that he was the class's best debater, even though he wasn't. But Lyndon, said a student, "had a knack of finding a weak point in the other team's argument and coming back at it pretty good."

He chatted with any professor who would stop to talk. Often he sat on the floor or the grass, staring upward as the professor talked. His mouth hung open as though he was amazed to hear such wisdom. "He would just drink up what they were saying," a student said, "sit at their knees and drink it up."

Professors liked this stringbean of a fellow who listened to them with such awe. And they saw how Prexy Evans, their boss, liked to listen to Lyndon. Maybe Lyndon would say something nice to Prexy about them. By his second semester, the summer of 1927, Lyndon was getting A's and B's.

One day, back in Johnson City, he threw his report card in front of his father. He pointed to the A's and said loudly, "Does that look like I've got enough sense for a college education?"

He had learned at nineteen what his father had never learned: "To get along, go along." Lyndon put it this way to the campus idol with whom he was so close that they were known as Johnson and Johnson: "Boody, the way you get ahead in the world, you get close to those that are the head of things, like Prexy Evans, for example."

Lyndon had borrowed so much money that he had to drop out of San Marcos for a year to earn money to pay his debts. He taught Mexican children at a school in a village in south Texas. In the fall of 1929 he came back for his last year at San Marcos. He still wanted to be an "in" Black Star. Again the Black Stars said no.

Another student, a fast-talking salesman type, Horace Richards, was jealous of the Black Stars because they dated the prettiest girls. So Horace formed another society, the White Stars. Maybe pretty girls would think White Stars were "in" too. "We had no thought of politics," he said later. "We did it because of the girls."

Lyndon joined the White Stars, but not because of the girls. He had seen how things worked at San Marcos. Black Stars voted for each other and were elected class officers and members of the student council. And Black Stars then got each other the college's best-paying jobs.

Lyndon convinced Horace that the White Stars should be secret. Members had to take an oath that they would not tell anyone about the society. They met at night by candlelight along the bank of a creek. At one meeting Lyndon suggested the White Stars put up a candidate for the president of the senior class.

"I bet it's you, huh, Lyndon," a boy said.

No, Lyndon said, too many students disliked him. "Let's take ole Bill," he drawled, pointing to Willard (Bill) Deason. "He's got no scars on him"—meaning he had no enemies.

Bill was nominated. The White Stars themselves laughed about his chances. Everyone knew that Dick Spinn, who was a Black Star and a handsome football hero, would win. Black Stars always won.

Lyndon told Horace and Bill Deason that Bill needed an "issue" to win. Lyndon had the issue. Students had to pay a "blanket tax," which was used mostly for the teams' athletic equipment. Only a tiny fraction of the money went to nonsports clubs, such as the debating team and music society.

Most students never voted, Lyndon had discovered. Only the Black Stars cared to be class officers. To make more students vote, Deason made speeches in which he demanded more money for the nonathletes, who greatly outnumbered the athletes. Bill's slogan was "Brains are just as important as brawn." Students nodded in agreement. On election day Bill Deason won, the victor in Lyndon's first political campaign.

The Black Stars were shocked. How could the popular Dick Spinn lose to a student no one knew? "The Black Stars didn't know we were organized," Bill Deason told Robert Caro years later. "*Nobody* knew. They didn't know that this was an *organization* working on them. They knew *someone* was playing havoc with the school, but they didn't know who."

Lyndon had won a campaign. Now he wanted to win an election. He told the White Stars to nominate him to be the senior-class representative on the student council. His opponent was a Black Star, Joe Berry. Joe, a football pass catcher, had replaced Boody, who had graduated, as the most popular man on campus. "We didn't think Lyndon had much of a chance," Horace Richards said, "but he wanted to be the representative and he wanted it bad."

Lyndon told Horace what the White Stars should do. Horace was the president of the White Stars and thought he was the leader. But Bill Deason saw that Lyndon had become the real leader, who put ideas into Horace's head and made Horace think they were his own.

Lyndon's idea was simple. All the White Stars—sophomores, juniors, and seniors—poured into the room where the seniors were voting. No one at San Marcos knew who was in what class. The White Stars cast their votes for Lyndon, then fled before they could be identified. They swarmed into another room where the juniors were voting. They voted for a White Star. Then they rushed to where the sophs were voting. They voted a third time—for, of course, a White Star.

Lyndon won, by a single vote. So did the other White Stars. Years later Horace Richards told Robert Caro, "I felt that I had been in on the beginning of history. Because I was in on the *first* election that Lyndon Johnson stole."

Students knew he was up to something. "He was always head-huddling people," one said. "He always had something they had to confer about."

But when arguments started, he walked away. He never took sides. If pressed, he said he hadn't made up his mind. When he talked to a professor who was a Republican, Lyndon seemed to agree with the professor. When he talked to a Democrat, he seemed to agree with the Democrat. One friend said, "Lyndon doesn't stand for anything."

Students discovered, however, that Lyndon was a good man to know. By the spring of 1930 the Great Depression had crippled America. Factories shut down. Jobless people stood on long lines to get a slice of bread and a bowl of soup. Students had to drop out of college. Their families couldn't pay the tuition.

A campus job kept the lucky ones in school. By 1930 Lyndon, Prexy's friend, had two of the best jobs. He was Prexy's office boy and the summer editor of the school paper. San Marcos deans knew how close Lyndon was to Prexy. "If Lyndon would say to [a dean], this boy is a good boy, give him a job, he'd get that job," Horace Richards said. Before 1930 only Black Stars had gotten the good jobs and won elections. In 1930 only White Stars got the good jobs and won elections.

One White Star needed help, but he said he would never ask Bull Johnson for anything. A friend told Lyndon that this White Star needed a job to stay in college.

"If he's got too much pride to ask me for a job," Lyndon said, "I ain't going to give him one. If he asks me, I'll give him anything I got. But he's got to ask."

The student asked. Lyndon got him a job. "Lyndon," Horace Richards said, "wanted to show off his power."

Years later Lyndon visited San Marcos. He talked of the Black Stars who had slammed a door in his face. "They lost everything I could have them lose," he said. "I broke their back good and it stayed broke a good long time."

In August 1930, the twenty-two-year-old Lyndon graduated. No professor had taught Lyndon what he had learned by himself: that people can be brought together as a group to do things they won't, or can't, do by themselves. He had learned how to be a politician.

5

Lady Bird

They had to help. Lyndon demanded that they help. And the White Stars came.

It was the fall of 1930, and Lyndon had been out of San Marcos for a month. A young lawyer, Welly Hopkins, was running for the state senate in Austin. He wanted to represent counties that included those in the Hill Country. He knew that Sam Johnson had never lost an election, so he asked Sam's son to campaign for him in the Hill Country. Lyndon phoned Bill Deason, Horace Richards, and other White Stars, reminding them that they had never lost an election in San Marcos. They came to Johnson City, then fanned out across the Hill Country. They handed out Welly Hopkins pamphlets. They spoke to people in towns and on farms.

Hopkins won every county in the Hill Country. When he went to Austin, he talked about the "wonder kid" from Johnson City who knew how to get votes.

Lyndon, meanwhile, needed a job. He was one of almost twenty million men and women unemployed in the Great Depression. He sent out dozens of letters seeking work as a teacher. He was one of the lucky few. A Houston high school hired him to teach debating. Until then, the school's debating team had nearly always lost. Lyndon taught two students, the stocky Gene Latimer and the tall Luther Jones, how to debate the same way his father had taught

The high-school debating teacher with his Sam Houston High School team of 1931. They almost won the state championship. The two girls are Margaret Epley (left) and Evelyn Lee. On the far left is Luther Jones, on the right Gene Latimer, both of whom would later work for Lyndon in Austin and Washington.

him to argue. Six months later Latimer and Jones came within one vote, 3–2, of winning the state's debating championship. Lyndon shook the hands of the two orators, then went backstage and threw up. *To come so close . . .*

He had a good job while many Texans were jobless and hungry. But he told friends he would never be a *somebody* as a teacher. Late in 1931, he got a call from Dick Kleberg, a millionaire rancher. A Democrat, Kleberg had just been elected to the United States House of Representatives, representing a district in south Texas that included Corpus Christi and San Antonio. Welly Hopkins had told Kleberg about the "wonder kid"; Kleberg asked Lyndon if he would take charge of his new congressional office in Washington. This job meant answering the letters sent to the congressman by voters. A stunned Lyndon quickly accepted.

"We were like two scared field mice when we started." That's how a nervous secretary described herself and Lyndon when they arrived in Washington to work for

Lyndon Johnson comes to Washington in 1931 as a congressman's assistant. Behind him is the Capitol, the home of the Congress, in which he would serve for most of the next thirty years.

Kleberg late in 1931. They stared at mountains of mailbags. Hundreds of letters poured in each day from Kleberg's vast district of 230,000 people. The letter writers begged for help. They wanted government pensions, jobs, and other kinds of aid in these depressed times.

Lyndon ripped open the letters. He hired Gene Latimer and Luther Jones, his two young orators, and sat them in front of typewriters. From dawn until close to midnight, they slaved over the keys, pounding out replies to those letters, promsing that Congressman Kleberg would help.

Lyndon sat at a desk, his willowy frame hunched over a phone. "Congressman Kleberg's office calling!" he shouted, talking to officials at government agencies. He needed a favor, he said, for a Kleberg constituent (meaning a voter). He pleaded and demanded, cajoled and threatened. If he got a no, he would slam down the phone and race down Capitol Hill; he'd storm into the agency's office and pound his large fists on desks. He would not leave until he got yes for an answer.

He told Latimer and Jones, "If you do absolutely everything you *could* do, you would succeed."

Latimer and Jones, only a few years younger, respectfully called him The Chief. They winced as he tongue-lashed them. "I hope your mind isn't as messy as that desk!" he shouted at Latimer one morning. Latimer pounded his typewriter, letters strewn in front of him. Within a few hours, all the letters were answered. Lyndon stared at the clean desk and snarled, "I hope your mind's not as empty as that desk!"

Latimer and Jones went on slaving. Lyndon's frantic drive and stormy rages seemed to hypnotize the people around him. "He can make you cry, he can make you laugh, he can do everything," Latimer once said. "You felt like 'I belong to him and he belongs to me.'" Both Jones and Latimer, and nearly all the people who ever worked for Lyndon, sensed that they were hitched to a rising star.

By late 1933, having been in Washington only two years, the once-scared mouse now strode the halls of Congress like a lion. Lyndon was the boss of the "Little Congress," which was made up of the assistants to congressmen. Members of the Little Congress debated bills, then voted to reject or pass them, just like members of the House.

Lyndon studied the rules for the Little Congress. Like the House, it was governed by a Speaker. Lyndon wanted to be elected Speaker. He made friends with elevator operators, guards, and other House employees. By the rules, they *could* be members of the Little Congress; the only reason they weren't members was that they hadn't paid the yearly dues. On the night of April 27, 1933, the Little Congress met to vote for a Speaker. Into the room flooded the elevator operators and guards. The congressmen's assistants gawked, surprised. Lyndon called for a vote. He was elected Speaker. He grabbed the gavel, banged it on the table, and announced that he was the Speaker of the Little Congress.

The next morning the assistants realized they had been tricked. Lyndon had gotten votes from people who were not members; they had not paid their dues. "He stole that election," one assistant growled, unaware that it was not the first.

Lyndon roamed the halls of Congress asking representatives and senators to speak to the Little Congress. He had an excuse, Gene Latimer once said, "to see Senator Huey Long or Tom Connolly, or a Texas Congressman who was the head of a committee.... Once he got in to see somebody ... The Chief, being the way he was, would make them remember him."

In the fall of 1934 Lyndon was traveling from Dick Kleberg's home office in Corpus Christi to Washington. He stopped in Austin to see friends. There, for the second time in his life, he met Claudia Alta Taylor.

Claudia Alta Taylor was the daughter of the richest man in Karnack, a small town in east Texas. Her father owned two grocery stores, a cotton gin, and thousands of acres. "Cap'n" Taylor lived in a mansion called The Brick House. Servants waited on his only daughter.

Claudia's mother had died when she was two. She had been raised by an aunt. A nurse named her Lady Bird because she was "as purty as a lady bird." A shy girl, she had few friends in high school. Often, at dances, she stood alone.

Lady Bird went to the University of Texas in Austin. She wanted to be either a teacher or a newspaper reporter. "I thought that people in the press went more places and met more interesting people and had more exciting things happen to them," she once told Robert Caro.

Slightly over five feet tall, dainty and slim, with dark hair and large eyes, she had a birdlike manner that fitted her nickname. She had a girlfriend who worked in Austin.

In 1933 Sam Johnson, by then working for the state as a bus inspector, met Lady Bird and introduced her to Lyndon. Lyndon asked for a date, but she said no.

A year later, in September 1934, Lyndon was chatting with friends in an Austin office when Lady Bird chanced to come by. He asked her to meet him the next morning in a coffee shop. She didn't say yes or no to him, but to herself she said that she was too busy to have coffee with anyone the next morning.

That morning, however, she had to walk by the shop. From a table Lyndon waved at her. She went in. He insisted that she go with him in his car for a ride in the country. Too stunned to say no, she slipped into the car. As he drove the car, whizzing by other cars, he threw dozens of questions at her about her family, her life, her goals. He talked about himself and how one day he would be a somebody. Her quick mind was aware that he was just as quick. "It could follow another mind around," someone once said, "and get there before it did."

Then, as he jerked the speeding car around slower cars, he asked her to marry him. She laughed, sure he was joking, and said no. But she thought he was "very good-looking with lots of black wavy hair."

The next day he took her to Johnson City to visit his parents. His father was a pale ghost of the once-fiery legislator. The mother, Lady Bird saw, was much like herself, one who admired good books, plays, and who enjoyed art and museums—"the higher and more beautiful things of life," as Rebekah often put it.

Lyndon again asked Lady Bird to marry him. She said no, but kissed him good-bye when he finally left for Washington. Later she told Robert Caro: "I knew I had met something remarkable, but I didn't know quite what. . . . I had a queer sort of moth-and-flame feeling."

He wrote to her every day, called twice a day. Yes, he assured her, he, too, loved the beautiful things—literature, drama, museums. He didn't say that he rarely opened a

Lyndon and Lady Bird pose for a photographer on their honeymoon in Mexico in November 1934. Six months earlier, she had known him only as a gangling young man who didn't seem interesting enough to date.

book and hadn't stepped inside a theater or museum in years. Early in November he phoned to tell her he was driving to Karnack from Washington.

The next morning Lady Bird awoke to hear a car's honk. She peered out the bedroom window and saw Lyndon. He had driven all day and all night the 1,200 miles to Karnack. Moments later he told her they should be married right away.

A bewildered Lady Bird said she had to talk it over with her friend in Austin. Lyndon told her they would drive to Austin. On the way he suddenly spun in the seat and said, "We either get married now or we never will. And if you say good-bye to me, it just proves to me that you don't love me enough to. And I just can't bear to go on and keep wondering if it will ever happen."

Lady Bird could not turn back that final appeal. That evening she walked down the aisle toward a waiting minister and a smiling Lyndon.

The newlyweds went to Washington where they moved into a one-bedroom apartment. Bird, as Lyndon would always call her, went to the city's libraries, museums, and theaters. She went alone. Lyndon was busy from early morning to as late as midnight answering mail.

Lady Bird arose each morning and served her husband coffee as he lay in bed scanning the morning newspaper. She put out his clothes. She inserted, at his order, a fountain pen in one pocket, handkerchief in another, wallet and keys in their proper places. She draped his knotted tie around a knob. He could grab it and fling it around his neck as he hurried out the door.

Once, at a party, he noticed she had a run in her stocking. He ordered her to leave the room and change the stocking. She dallied, talking to someone. "Now! Bird! Now!" Lyndon roared. She hurried from the room. People said to each other about the woman who had been waited upon by servants, "How does she stand it?" She stood it because, like Gene Latimer and all of Lyndon's other willing slaves, she did it for *him*, that hypnotizing storm.

By now the boss of the Little Congress had met a great many of Washington's most important people. In 1933 Franklin Delano Roosevelt, the former governor of New York, had become the nation's president. A Democrat, he told a near-bankrupt, frightened nation that all it had to fear "is fear itself." He promised a "New Deal" that would help businessmen to make profits, workers to get jobs, and farmers to get higher prices for their crops.

During his first months in office, F.D.R. (as the newspapers called the president) asked Congress to pass laws to give Americans that New Deal. A majority of congressmen and senators were Democrats. They joined with some Republicans to pass laws that created agencies to help businessmen, workers, and farmers. Among the agencies were the Public Works Administration (PWA), Works Progress Administration (WPA), Civilian Conservation Corps (CCC), and Agricultural Administration Agency (AAA). These agencies had millions of dollars to distribute to jobless workers and bankrupt farmers.

Many Republicans and Democrats argued that it was

"communistic" for the government to hand out money to people. But money now jingled in the pockets of more and more Americans, who spent it on food, clothes, and other necessities. Farmers got higher prices for their produce. Factories hired workers so they could turn out goods to replace those being sold in stores. More men and women had jobs—and money to spend.

One of F.D.R.'s most enthusiastic supporters in the House of Representatives was a stumpy, balding man who had once stood next to Sam Ealy Johnson in the Texas House— Sam Rayburn. He battled banks and railroads to get lower interest rates and lower freight charges. Mr. Sam, as people in north Texas called him, was a bachelor. On weekends, while other congressmen laughed with their families, Mr. Sam walked the empty streets of Washington alone. People predicted he would rise to become Speaker of the House— his ambition since he had been a boy on a farm. Even now, in 1934, other congressmen spoke respectfully of his fifteen years of work in the House. But on weekends he was just another lonely man.

He knew Sam Johnson's son and welcomed him to Washington. Lyndon kissed Mr. Sam on his bald dome. Other congressmen, who tiptoed around Mr. Sam when he got angry, stared at this display of affection and were shocked. But Mr. Sam's gruffness seemed to melt away when Lyndon came around.

Lyndon often sat at Mr. Sam's feet as Rayburn talked about New Deal bills being debated in Congress. Lyndon stared up at Mr. Sam with the same awe he had shown to San Marcos professors. Sam looked down at the adoring Lyndon with the fondness of a father.

Once, when Lyndon was stricken by pneumonia, Mr. Sam rushed from the House to sit by his side until Lyndon's fever fell. When Lyndon awoke, he saw the anxious face of Mr. Sam, who told him, "Don't you worry... if you need money or anything, just call on me."

6

Stepping Stones

Alvin Wirtz was calling. Lyndon Johnson knew who Alvin Wirtz was. He quickly picked up the telephone and asked Alvin Wirtz what Congressman Kleberg's office could do for him.

"Senator" Wirtz, as Texas politicians called him, was a lawyer in Austin for oil, gas, and construction companies. One of his jobs was getting politicians to pass laws that would keep down taxes businessmen had to pay. He talked Texas legislators into passing such laws. When a legislator said no to Alvin Wirtz, the legislator might come back from a vacation to find that Alvin's friends had passed a law changing his district. In the next election that legislator would lose.

Wirtz came to Washington in 1935 to seek money for one of his clients, Herman Brown, head of the Brown & Root construction company. Brown wanted to build a dam in the Texas Hill Country with some of the millions of dollars available from New Deal agencies. Wirtz called Congressman Kleberg's office to ask whom he should see in Washington. As usual, Kleberg was out on the golf course. Wirtz talked to Lyndon. Could Lyndon get him appointments with New Deal officials?

Lyndon called agency officials. Most knew him, and knew that he and Mr. Sam were close. They knew, too, that Mr. Sam and his allies decided how much money the agencies would get each year from the treasury. Agency officials were always anxious to please Mr. Sam—and any friend of his.

That evening Lyndon called Wirtz at his hotel. Wirtz could see all the officials he wanted to see.

Wirtz was still amazed when he went back to Austin. He told his wealthy clients that Lyndon "knew Washington. He could get you into any place."

Lyndon, however, felt trapped in Kleberg's office. He could never be a somebody as an assistant. Meanwhile, Kleberg was bored with his own job. He wanted to be the ambassador to Mexico, a country he loved. Lyndon asked Mr. Sam to talk the president into making Kleberg the ambassador to Mexico. Then Lyndon could run for his seat. But someone else got the ambassador's job.

In 1935 F.D.R. set up a new agency, the National Youth Administration (NYA). The NYA's mission was to put young people to work so they could stay in school or work on projects after they left school. Each state would have its own NYA director.

Lyndon asked a White House official to make him the Texas NYA director. The official laughed. At twenty-eight, Lyndon was too young. Lyndon called Sam Rayburn. Mr. Sam put on his hat and walked to the White House. Lyndon got the job.

He and Lady Bird flew to Austin. He phoned former White Stars, such as Bill Deason. Lyndon had gotten a job for Deason with a federal bank, and that job, Bill said, was the best he'd ever had. Bill had never heard of the NYA. But Bill and dozens of other White Stars came to the NYA to slave for Lyndon. So did others who had asked Kleberg's help in getting government jobs. Grateful to Lyndon, they joined the NYA.

But it was not only gratefulness that made them come. "I'm working for the greatest chief in the world," one man exulted. "Someday he's going to be president of the United States."

Gene Latimer and Luther Jones, Lyndon's old high-school orators, came from Washington. "You felt," Jones said, " ... that whatever he ran for, he would win."

At first, however, the new state director was scared. He would be the boss of thousands of workers. He had to start from nothing. Could he do the job? He nervously twisted his long fingers as he shouted to assistants and dictated letters. Later, remembering how nervous Lyndon had been, Lady Bird told Robert Caro, "Lyndon was not the supremely confident person he seemed, you know."

He shook off his doubts. Cursing and ranting at his staff, he told them, "We have a job to help poor boys and girls—let's put the kids to work!" Within a few months, thousands of young Texans were building roadside rest parks. Others, after classes, aided teachers and librarians.

Alvin Wirtz's office was near Lyndon's. Wirtz had never forgotten how Lyndon "knew Washington." Like most older men, he was fascinated by Lyndon. As a Texas politician once said, Lyndon could stop an older man in the street, "and in five minutes he could get that man to think. 'I like you, young fellow, I'll be for you.'"

Like Mr. Sam, Wirtz began to admire Lyndon as a father would. He had no son of his own. On a photo of himself, he wrote, "To Lyndon Johnson, who I ... love as if he were in fact my son."

With Mr. Sam, Lyndon had a "daddy" who had power in Washington. Now he had another "daddy," one who had power in Texas.

Wirtz, meanwhile, was worried about his client Herman Brown. Brown & Root had begun to build the dam in the Hill Country for the government. Brown spent his life's savings, a half million dollars, for work on the dam. His contract said he would get the money back—and much more—when the dam was built. But late in 1936, an official in Washington ruled that the contract was illegal. The dam was being built on land not owned by the U.S. Government. By law, all U.S. dams had to be built on land the government owned. Herman Brown stood to lose half a million dollars. He would be ruined.

Alvin Wirtz called Congressman James Buchanan (known as "Buck"). The dam was being built in Buck's Tenth Congressional District. Buck told Wirtz not to worry. In early 1937, he said, he would slip a bill through Congress making the dam legal.

Then, in February 1937, Buck Buchanan suddenly had a heart attack and died. His bill, without his push, would not go through Congress.

When Lyndon read that Buchanan had died, he barged into Wirtz's office. He said that this was his chance—he would run for Buchanan's seat as the congressman from the Hill Country. Would Alvin help him?

Wirtz had to hesitate. True, this was his "adopted" son. But almost everyone in Austin expected the widow of the popular Buck to run for the seat and win. Wirtz didn't want a congresswoman mad at him.

But he also had to think: Could Buck's widow get that bill through Congress to make the dam legal? Not likely. But here, sitting anxiously in front of him, was someone who knew how to get things done in Washington.

He would back Lyndon, he said. Then he told Lyndon how to win.

7

"Will You Give Me Your Hand?"

Lyndon scanned the front page of the newspaper. As he read, a friend said later, "You could see the color drain out of his face, he went white as a sheet."

Lyndon had just read that Buck Buchanan's widow seemed ready to run. The newspaper writer said she would almost certainly win.

The next morning Lyndon knocked at the house of the man who had first taught him politics. Sam Johnson was bent and pale, but the old pol's eyes glittered when he heard that Lyndon wanted to run for Congress. Lyndon said he was worried about Mrs. Buchanan.

"What do you mean?" Sam snapped. "If she knows she's going to have a fight, she won't run. Announce now—before she announces. If you do, she won't run."

Hours later, Lyndon told reporters he would run. The next day Mrs. Buchanan said she would not run.

Alvin Wirtz told Lyndon how to campaign. F.D.R.'s New Deal agencies had put money in the pockets of Texas farmers and workers. Some conservative Democrats, including those who would be running for Buchanan's seat, had criticized F.D.R. They called him a dictator who was trying to put Congress and the Supreme Court in the backseat and drive the government all by himself.

To Texans, Wirtz told Lyndon, "F.D.R. is God." And he added, "You go out and you say over and over, 'Roosevelt, Roosevelt, Roosevelt.'"

Lyndon nodded. He was the man "who had never stood for anything" in San Marcos. When he had talked to New Deal Democrats in Washington or Austin, he had always agreed with them. But when he talked to conservative Democrats, he agreed with them. One summer, as Kleberg's assistant, he had led the campaign of a Texas Democrat who was a New Dealer. Then he had led the campaign of another Texan who was a conservative.

"I don't think Lyndon was a conservative or a liberal," Luther Jones once said. "I think he was what he felt like he needed to be. . . . He could become either an ultra-liberal or an ultra-conservative if that would have brought victory. . . . Winning is the name of the game."

Buchanan's Tenth Congressional District was bigger than the states of Connecticut and Delaware put together. It contained almost 250,000 people. Lyndon knew his opponents would win in the cities, such as Austin and Lockhart. Lyndon had to win the small villages and farms of the Hill Country.

Working for him were several White Stars—Bill Deason for one—and Washington aides, among them Luther Jones. He had his NYA staff workers. And he had dozens of men and women who had federal jobs that Lyndon had gotten for them. Those people campaigned for Lyndon all across the Hill Country and the other farming areas of the vast district.

Lyndon's hardest worker was himself. Before dawn he flopped into his limousine. His chauffeur drove him to distant villages and farms as the sun rose. Lyndon walked across furrowed fields to talk to a single man behind a plow. He grabbed the man's overalls and said, "Listen, I'm running for Congress. I need help. I want your vote. Will

A gaunt Lyndon, black smudges under his eyes after more than a month of exhausting campaigning, towers above a group of supporters during his first campaign for public office.

you help me? Will you give me your hand?" He stuck out his hand, staring nose to nose into the farmer's face.

In the heat of the spring sun, he stood in front of three or four men on a hillside and shouted, "What president ever cared about the farmer before Mr. Roosevelt? He was for the poor man. He wanted the farmers to have a break. And he gave 'em a break. He gave *us* a break."

He spoke of how F.D.R. was being opposed in Congress. "Mr. Roosevelt's in trouble now. When we needed help, he helped us. Now *he* needs help. Are you going to give it to him? By electing Lyndon Johnson?" That, he said, "is what this election is all about."

Alvin Wirtz, meanwhile, was collecting money for the campaign from his rich clients. Lyndon bought time to speak on radio. He bought ads in weekly papers, ads that led to favorable articles about him. He paid for beef-and-beer barbecues. Voters were told to "eat and drink all you want—it's on Lyndon."

Like the other candidates, Lyndon bought votes. Lead men in poor black and Mexican-American communities were given a dollar or two for each vote they could deliver.

Still, the newspaper polls showed that he was no better than fourth in the seven-man field. Lyndon read the polls and snarled at campaign workers, "You cost me fifty votes with that mistake you made today in Brenham. You really cut a knife into me in Brenham, didn't you? You just cut it in and twisted it." Other workers cringed as his smudged eyes swept the room.

By early April—the special election was on April 10—Lyndon had traveled ten miles for each mile covered by his opponents. He had campaigned every day while they spoke mostly on Saturdays. He had spent almost $100,000 of Alvin Wirtz's money, at least twice what any opponent had spent. But he was still behind in the polls.

But the poll takers hadn't gone deep into the countryside. There, night after night, when Lyndon shouted to a handful of farmers or villagers, "Roosevelt! Roosevelt! Roosevelt!" the audience chanted, "Roosevelt and Johnson! Roosevelt and Johnson! Roosevelt and Johnson!"

Those dawn-to-midnight trips exhausted him. Jacket and pants hung on an emaciated frame, his weight down from 160 to 140. His face was drawn and pale.

Two days before the election, pain twisted his face as he tried to make a speech. He went to a hospital, where doctors cut out an inflamed appendix. For two days he had to lie silent, fists clenched in anger and frustration, as opponents campaigned.

On election day, the votes began to trickle in. Lyndon was in fourth place after the votes from Austin and other cities were counted. Then the votes began to come in from the villages and farms. Lyndon rose to third, to second— and then he flashed ahead.

He won with some 8,000 votes. His nearest opponent had only 5,000. Lyndon was the winner of his first race. At only twenty-nine, he was one of the nation's youngest congressmen. And the president of the United States wanted to meet him.

8

"I'll Go to the President!"

President Roosevelt shook Lyndon's hand as they stood on the Galveston dock. F.D.R. had been cruising in his yacht off the Texas coast. He had been told about the tall Texan who was campaigning, "Roosevelt! Roosevelt! Roosevelt!" His aides told Lyndon to come to Galveston to meet the president when the president's yacht docked.

F.D.R. invited Lyndon to ride in his special train that was taking him back to Washington. For hours, as the train rolled across the plains, the president and Lyndon chatted. Like most older men, the president liked Lyndon. "It seemed," an observer once said about those older men, "that Lyndon knew what they were thinking before they thought it. So he was always telling them exactly what they themselves were thinking."

Lyndon left the train in Austin. When the president arrived in Washington, he told his New Dealers that Lyndon could be "the twentieth century's first southern president." He told others, "I've just met the most remarkable young man. Now I like this boy, and you're going to help him with anything you can."

President Roosevelt shakes the hand of the new congress-
man who campaigned successfully by repeating over and
over, "Roosevelt! Roosevelt! Roosevelt!" Between them is
Texas Governor James Allred. This photo, with the governor
air-brushed out, was later blown up bigger than life-size and
posted on billboards across Texas when Lyndon ran for the
Senate in 1941.

When Lyndon and Lady Bird arrived in Washington, the heads of New Deal agencies invited them to their parties. They wanted to meet the young man F.D.R. was raving about.

One of the most powerful men in Washington was Tommy Corcoran (known as "the Cork"). He could whisper a word into F.D.R.'s ear and an official would be fired. When the Cork called an agency and said, "This is Tommy Corcoran at the White House," knees shook.

Lyndon had come to Washington knowing that Alvin Wirtz and Herman Brown needed a law to make the dam legal. Lyndon asked the Cork if he could help get the bill through Congress. The Cork talked to the president, who said, "Give the kid the dam."

Democrats rushed the bill through the House and Senate. The president signed it into law. The president's son told Alvin Wirtz, "We are doing this for Congressman Johnson."

Herman Brown was saved from ruin. He was grateful. He told Lyndon that if he ever wanted *anything*, Lyndon had it just for the asking.

Lyndon would ask.

Lyndon ran his office the way he had run Dick Kleberg's office. When a voter sent him a letter, his busy staff typed a reply that promised quick results. New Deal agency officials were anxious to please Lyndon, knowing he was close to Sam Rayburn. And they knew how F.D.R. had raved about him. When Lyndon asked an agency to do something for a Tenth District voter, more often than not it was done. WPA workers built a new high school in Johnson City. Hill Country farmers got loans at low interest rates. In 1938, when he'd been a congressman only two years, Lyndon "got more projects and more money for his district than anybody else," Tommy Corcoran told New Dealers.

"I'll get it for you!" Lyndon growled. "I'll go to the president if I have to." A group of Hill Country farmers had just asked him to get a loan from a federal agency. They needed the loan to string electric wires into the Hill Country. Then their kids could read under bulbs instead of flickering kerosene lamps. They could listen to a radio for the first time in their lives. Wives could have washing machines; farmers could have water pumps to irrigate their land.

A federal agency had turned down the farmers when they asked for the loan. Lyndon went to the White House. He told the president how poor the people of the Hill Country were. The president picked up a phone and told an agency chief to approve the loan.

Hill Country men, women, and children put up the poles and strung the wire. They were paid three dollars a day—a huge sum in those times. And when the lights went on all over the once-dark Hill Country, a newspaper editor said, "It was about then that Hill Country people began to name their kids for Lyndon Baines Johnson."

Roosevelt and his vice president, Jack Garner, a Texan, were quarreling. F.D.R. wanted to run for a third term in 1940. No President had ever run for three terms. Conservatives, such as "Cactus" Jack Garner, worried that F.D.R. wanted to be president for life. "He'll really be a dictator," they said, "just like that Adolf Hitler who is terrorizing Europe."

Jack Garner decided to run against F.D.R. for the Democratic nomination. Texans rallied around their favorite son—Cactus Jack.

As the new Speaker of the House, Sam Rayburn was very close to F.D.R. The president called him almost every day for advice. Sam didn't want to have to choose between his fellow Texan, Cactus Jack, and F.D.R. But if he had to choose, he knew he would pick his friend Cactus Jack. Of Sam it was said, "If he is your friend, he is your friend forever."

Sam was the White House's number-one Texas Democrat. If a man wanted a high-paying federal job in Texas, he went to see Sam. If Sam said O.K., the White House said O.K. If Sam said no, the White House said no. Sam knew that if he came out in favor of Cactus Jack, he would no longer be the White House's number-one Texas Democrat.

Lyndon wanted to be that number-one Texas Democrat. He would never be a somebody as a junior congressman. He knew that Sam Rayburn had waited twenty years to grasp the power of House Speaker. Lyndon, impatient to get ahead, couldn't wait that long.

He and Alvin Wirtz had an idea. They told people in Texas to send a telegram to Sam demanding that he

The young congressman in his Washington office, a photo of F.D.R., the most important man in his life on one side, a photo of the most important woman in his life, the lady he called Bird, on the other.

support Garner against F.D.R. Sam sent back a wire saying simply that all Texans should support a favorite son like Garner. Someone showed the telegram to a Texas reporter. The next day, across Texas, headlines blared: RAYBURN FOR GARNER.

In the White House F.D.R. and his aides frowned.

By late 1939 Garner knew he could not beat F.D.R. World War II had flared all across Europe. Americans were building planes and ships and training soldiers for defense in case the nation was attacked. Most Democrats wanted an experienced commander-in-chief. That meant F.D.R.

Roosevelt picked a new vice president, Henry Wallace, to run with him in the 1940 election. The president worried that the Democrats, especially those running for House seats, didn't have enough money to beat Republicans. He feared that even if he won a third term, he could not get any of his bills through a Congress filled with Republicans.

Lyndon knew F.D.R. was worried. In the fall of 1940, he called his friend Herman Brown. Lyndon had just helped Herman to get a $50 million contract to build a naval base in Texas. The grateful Herman told Lyndon that he and his rich friends would send all the money Lyndon asked for. As the money poured in, Lyndon doled it out to House Democrats running for reelection.

Many of those Democrats disliked Lyndon. He was loud and a braggart. Worse, he got favors from New Deal agencies for businessmen in other congressmen's districts. The businessmen called Lyndon and ignored their own congressmen. Those congressmen were furious.

But now they thanked Lyndon as he sent them money. He sent money to those he liked and thought would win. To others, despite their frantic pleas, he sent nothing.

On election night F.D.R. learned quickly that he had won a third term. He phoned Lyndon to see how his House Democrats were doing. "How many seats have the

Democrats lost?" he asked anxiously. Lyndon happily told him the Democrats would *gain* seats.

Roosevelt was delighted and impressed. So were some thirty to forty Democrats who had won because of Lyndon's money. "When Lyndon called on them for a favor," one writer said, "he could count on them for whatever he wanted.... A lot of guys knew they might need him someday."

Now Lyndon was the White House's number-one Texas Democrat. When an agency was slow in approving a job for one of Lyndon's voters, the agency got a call from Tommy Corcoran: "Congressman Johnson wants this today, and the White House wants him to have it today." Herman Brown got more money to build military bases. Alvin Wirtz was appointed to the number-two job in the Department of Interior.

9

"Sit on the Ballot Boxes"

"Are you backing Lyndon Johnson for the Senate, Mr. President?"

The president flashed his famous grin at the reporters. The reporters were standing in his office on an April day in 1941. "All I can say," the president said, "is Lyndon Johnson is a very old, old friend of mine."

Texas Senator Morris Sheppard had suddenly died. Just as he had done after Buck Buchanan's death, Lyndon rushed to talk to Alvin Wirtz after hearing the news. They talked to Herman Brown, who promised money.

Lyndon was thirty-two. He was still thin in the shoulders, but his middle was showing a paunch. His shiny black hair contrasted with pale white skin. He wore gold-rimmed glasses. And as he talked to reporters on the steps of the White House, saying he would run for the Senate "under the banner of Roosevelt," he talked in the stately tones of an ambassador. Reporters wrote that he looked closer to forty than thirty.

At first Lyndon seemed the likely winner, being F.D.R.'s favorite. But then Governor Lee "Pappy" O'Daniel decided to run. A hillbilly singer, Pappy was the most popular man in Texas. He promised pension money to the old and poor. Twice he had been elected governor.

Like his father (who had died of a heart attack at sixty-one a few years earlier) Lyndon often took to his bed when bad news came. "Nervous exhaustion," newspapers said. "He was depressed," Lady Bird later said. For two weeks he stayed in a hospital while Pappy and his hillbilly band drew huge crowds.

Lyndon came out thin and pale. But no longer did he speak like a statesman. He waved wires from F.D.R. and read them to crowds: "Dear Lyndon, I have your letter favoring further help for senior citizens...." That meant pension money, Lyndon said. He could promise anything that Pappy promised.

Both Pappy and Lyndon bought votes from lead men. Pappy bought his in east Texas; Lyndon bought his in south Texas.

Each got almost the same number of votes on election night. By the next day, votes still trickling in, Lyndon crept out to a slight lead. A Johnson campaign worker got a call from south Texas: Should all those bought votes be announced now? Sure, said the campaign worker. Those votes would push Lyndon so far ahead he couldn't be caught.

A blunder had been made. As soon as all the south Texas votes were announced, Pappy O'Daniel's men knew exactly how many votes they needed from east Texas to win.

Sure enough, in came a flood of votes from east Texas for Pappy. He won, 175,590 to Lyndon's 174,279, a whisker-thin margin of 1,311 out of nearly 350,000 votes.

Lyndon knew the election had been stolen from his hands. He raged, white-faced, at his aides. He returned to Washington as a congressman.

FDR teased him: "In New York, we know enough to sit on the ballot boxes until they are counted."

Lyndon said nothing, but now he knew that crying "Roosevelt! Roosevelt! Roosevelt!" didn't mean victory anymore. Texas was changing. Maybe he would also have to change.

10

"You Must Be Crazy, Sir!"

Lieutenant Commander Lyndon Johnson climbed into the B-26 bomber. The plane's twin engines coughed in the murky morning light. The engines of other B-26s began to roar. They were lined up on an Army Air Corps landing strip in Australia. Their noses were pointed toward a Japanese island air base in the Pacific Ocean.

On December 7, 1941, Japanese planes had bombed the American naval base at Pearl Harbor in Hawaii. The United States Congress had declared war on Japan and its ally, Adolf Hitler's Germany. Within minutes after the declaration of war, Lyndon rose to ask the Speaker, Sam Rayburn, for a leave of absence. He was joining the U.S. Navy.

F.D.R. asked the new lieutenant commander to go to Australia. Japanese battlewagons and troops had rapidly spread west toward India. Many Americans feared the battlewagons would soon be shelling Los Angeles and San Francisco. F.D.R. asked Lyndon to see what the South Pacific Theater commander, General Douglas MacArthur, needed to turn back the Japanese tide.

Lieutenant Commander Johnson arrives at an air-force base in the southwest Pacific and is greeted by two generals. As an emissary from the president, Lyndon was treated as a VIP (Very Important Person).

In Australia Lyndon decided to fly on a B-26 mission to bomb a Japanese base. He climbed into one plane, nicknamed the Wabash Cannonball, but there was no space for him. He jumped out and climbed into another B-26, the Heckling Hare.

As the Heckling Hare climbed over the shimmering Pacific, a tail gunner asked him what a naval officer was doing in an Air Corps bomber.

Lyndon explained that he was a congressman. "You must be crazy, sir!" the gunner said. "This ain't no milk run, believe me. You don't need to come along and get shot up to find out about conditions here.... We'll *tell* you that."

The B-26 suddenly faltered. A generator had conked out, slowing the plane. Minutes later a gunner shouted, "Zeroes!" Japanese fighters swooped in on the wobbling Heckling Hare and the diving Wabash Cannonball. Bullets chewed at the wings of the Cannonball. It spiraled into the ocean and blew apart.

Lyndon had no time to glance downward at the oil-slicked grave. Bullets slammed into the Heckling Hare. The bomber's pilot kicked at the controls to evade those fiery bits of death.

A radioman, Corporal Lillis Walker, swayed with Lyndon in the tossing plane. "Boy, it's rough up here," Lyndon said.

Lillis nodded. He was surprised the passenger seemed so calm.

"You get kind of scared, don't you?" Lyndon asked.

"Yeah, I'm always scared up here."

Lyndon laughed. "I'm sure," Lillis said later, "he felt exactly the way I did, but he didn't show it a bit."

The Heckling Hare wobbled home to land safely, pocked with bullet holes. General MacArthur pinned the Silver Star medal on Lyndon's chest. It was a high award, one few airmen got even after twenty-five perilous missions. Lyndon knew MacArthur wanted to flatter a congressman close to the commander-in-chief. He thought about returning the Silver Star. Yet he knew that Texas voters revered the brave. He kept the medal and wore a silver star ribbon in his lapel for the rest of his life.

In Washington, meanwhile, the president ordered all congressmen to leave the military service. They would work for victory, he said, in the Congress.

Lady Bird had overseen the Tenth Congressional District office while Lyndon was away. She had proved to herself that she was a brisk and efficient executive. She decided to see what else she could manage. She had inherited about $50,000 from her father. KTBC, a small radio station in Austin, was for sale for $22,000. The station lost money, but Austin businesspeople told her it was run by weak hands.

Lady Bird bought the station. She got down on her knees and cleaned its hallways and grimy studios. She hired new executives. Some had worked for Lyndon in Austin at the NYA. They included Jesse Kellam, a former White Star.

Lyndon went to New York and talked the CBS Radio Network into making KTBC a CBS affiliate. CBS had no station in Austin. It made sense for CBS to have one. But network executives also knew a congressman's wife owned the station. The network was supervised by a federal agency, the Federal Communications Commission. It wouldn't hurt to have an affiliate that was owned by the wife of a congressman.

Soon the little 250-watt KTBC broadcast CBS shows such as *The Jack Benny Hour,* one of the nation's most popular. Many people in Austin tuned in to KTBC for the first time. Advertisers bought time. By late 1944, the station was worth about $100,000. And Lady Bird and Lyndon knew what was coming after the war to the broadcasting business: television.

On March 19, 1944, Lady Bird gave birth to a girl, "a red, crying, screaming baby girl," as the glowing father exulted. He demanded that nurses show him the baby immediately after the delivery. And after viewing the baby, he ran to a phone to call Sam Rayburn. His "daddy" was now a granddaddy.

Mr. Sam knew that Lyndon had tricked him by painting him into a corner with Cactus Jack Garner in 1940. That trick had cost Sam the warm friendship he'd once enjoyed with F.D.R. No longer was Sam number one in Texas. Lyndon was number one.

Sam had been furious. For months he had not spoken to the man he had looked upon as a son and promised "anything." He told intimates, "I don't know anyone who

The bald Sam Rayburn shakes hands with Lyndon. Johnson often shocked other congressmen, who feared the hard-bitten Mr. Sam, by kissing the Speaker on the top of his head.

is as vain or selfish as Lyndon Johnson." He talked scornfully of Lyndon's "arrogance" and "exhibitionism."

But no one else could talk scornfully about Lyndon within his hearing. He still boasted about how Lyndon had spooned out money to win seats for House Democrats in 1940 and again in 1942. Without those seats, Sam would not be Speaker—his lifelong dream. Sam owed a debt to Lyndon. Loyal Sam always paid his debts. And he still felt a father's love for Lyndon—though never after Lyndon's trick would it be a blind love.

Once again Sam was a Sunday visitor to the Johnsons' apartment. He brought toys for the new baby, who was named Lynda Bird after both her parents. Except on those Sundays, the dark-eyed baby saw little of her father. He raced off for Capitol Hill before she awoke in the morning, and often came home near midnight as she slept. But she heard a lot of talk of politics. At the age of three—so went a family joke—she knew what the word *constituent* meant.

"He was like a daddy to me always."

Lyndon was speaking to a *New York Times* reporter on the morning of April 12, 1945. Sam Rayburn had phoned Lyndon minutes earlier to tell him that President Roosevelt had died suddenly of a stroke. The new president was Harry S Truman, a former senator from Missouri, whom F.D.R. had picked as his vice-presidential running mate in 1944.

"I have seen the president in all kinds of moods, at breakfast, at lunch, at dinner," Lyndon told the reporter. "And never once in my five terms did he ever ask me to vote a certain way.... And when I voted against him—as I have plenty of times—he never said a word."

Actually, Lyndon had seldom voted against F.D.R. Until now he had been a loyal New Dealer. Lyndon was flashing a signal back to certain rich and powerful Texans. Lyndon's signal was a simple one: *I am with you.*

11

"Landslide Lyndon"

The Johnson City Windmill clattered down onto the football field on a sunny October day in 1948. Some 10,000 people sat in the stands, staring open-mouthed. Many had never seen a helicopter hover for a landing.

From the sky a voice roared from the craft's public-address system: "This is Lyndon Johnson, your next United States Senator, and I'll land in just a few minutes. I want to shake hands with all of you."

Herman Brown, now a multimillionaire after building World War II bases, had helped to buy the copter for Johnson. Lyndon was speeding across Texas in the craft to win the U.S. Senate election stolen from him in 1941. Pappy O'Daniel had gone back to Texas. This time Lyndon had to give up his House seat to run for the Senate, because it was a regular election. If he lost, his political career might be smashed.

Lyndon was desperate. No longer could he shout, "Roosevelt! Roosevelt! Roosevelt!" and expect to win. Oil and gas millionaires in Texas thought that the New Deal agencies were too strict in the ways they made businessmen obey federal rules. And they argued that the New Deal had built up labor unions to a size that made them bigger than corporations or even the government. Businessmen demanded laws to weaken the unions.

In 1946 the Republicans took control of the House and Senate. Sam Rayburn had to hand over his Speaker's gavel to a Republican. The Republicans, aided by conservative Democrats, put up a bill to limit the power of unions. It was named the Taft-Hartley bill, after its two Republican authors. Roosevelt New Dealers and Truman's new Fair Deal administration argued against the bill in Congress. Lyndon sat silent. One congressman said, "Lyndon leans with the wind."

Certainly, Lyndon saw which way the wind was blowing in Texas — toward conservativism, away from liberalism. He walked away from the New Dealers and voted for the Taft-Hartley bill, which became law in 1947.

He had sent a signal to Texans that he was no longer a liberal New Dealer. Liberals could no longer win in Texas. When an aide once told Lyndon that he ought to support a liberal civil-rights bill, the congressman stared at him disdainfully and said, "You couldn't get elected dogcatcher in Blanco County."

Now, supported by conservatives, Lyndon fluttered over Texas in his helicopter to try to become a senator. As cows and farmers stared upward in awe, he bellowed over the speaker, "This is your friend Lyndon Johnson. I'm sorry we can't land in your area today. But I want you to know I am up here thinking of you and appreciate your kind letters and comments. I just want you to be sure to tell your friends to vote for me at election time."

The favorite to win the Democratic nomination was Governor Coke Stevenson. (Republicans rarely won in Texas or anywhere in the South, so winning the Democratic nomination almost always meant election.) Stevenson got 45 percent of the votes, Lyndon 34 percent. Since neither got 51 percent, there had to be a runoff.

Friends advised Lyndon not to try too hard in the runoff. He'd waste his money, they said. Stevenson was too far ahead.

Lyndon hung his head. He was "as depressed as I have ever seen him," said Walter Jenkins, his secretary since 1940. But another aide, John Connally, told him he could win.

Lyndon shrugged and said he would try. But when he spoke, he seemed to have lost his confidence. Often he stumbled over words as he read his speeches.

Then he and Connally had an idea. The labor unions supported Coke Stevenson. Lyndon told cheering audiences that he had voted for Taft-Hartley, the bill to limit the unions' power. He asked, "Would Stevenson have voted for the law?" Stevenson was trapped. He couldn't say yes — the labor unions would be angry. He couldn't say no — his conservative supporters would be angry. He had to dodge the question. Many Texans who were unhappy about union power began to lean toward voting for Lyndon.

On election day, almost a million Texans voted. That night each candidate had about 50 percent. Eight days later, votes still trickling in, neither led by more than a hundred votes.

On the tenth day, a batch of 202 votes came in from Alice, a tiny town in south Texas. Of the 202 votes, 200 were for Lyndon. Those 200 pushed Lyndon ahead. In an election where almost a million votes were counted, Lyndon won by 87 votes.

Stevenson cried, "Foul play!" The Alice votes were checked. The 202 votes had been written onto the ballots in the same handwriting and with the same-color ink. A Stevenson aide talked to 11 of the 202 voters. None of the 11 had voted.

Stevenson suspected what had happened. Many of the votes in south Texas had been bought by a local power, George Parr. Parr did not like Coke Stevenson.

Stevenson went to a judge and tried to have Lyndon's name taken off the ballot for the general election. But, after months of legal wrangling, Lyndon was declared the winner—by those 87 votes. When he got to Washington in 1949 and took his seat in the Senate, Lyndon was teased by fellow Democrats, who called him Landslide Lyndon.

Others talked darkly of Lyndon's "stolen" election, a mirror image of the election stolen from him in 1941. Stolen election or not, Lyndon's political career had survived by a hair.

12

Uncle Dick and Hubert

The two little girls, a six-year-old and a three-year-old, skipped into the senator's office. They ran toward the tall, graying senator, who welcomed them with open arms. "Uncle Dick!" the girls shrieked. "Uncle Dick!"

Behind the girls walked their smiling father, Lyndon. Lynda Bird's little sister, Lucie Baines (who later changed the spelling to Luci), had been born on July 2, 1947. She was named for her aunt Lucia, Lyndon's sister. "Now all four of us have the same initials," Lyndon often said. "We save money by having the same initials on our luggage."

"Uncle Dick" was Richard Russell of Georgia, a Democratic senator. He was the leader of the conservatives in Congress.

Opposing senior conservatives like Russell, as the Congress opened in 1949, was a bunch of freshmen liberal senators. They included Minnesota's Hubert Humphrey, Tennessee's Estes Kefauver, and Illinois's Paul Douglas. In the fall of 1948, Harry Truman had campaigned for reelection by assailing the "do-nothing Congress." People shouted back, "Give them hell, Harry!" Harry was supposed to lose. Instead, he stunned the country by winning. And he brought with him to Washington enough Democratic

Lyndon's ability to get along with both liberals and conservatives all during his life is symbolized in this photo. On the left is Hubert Humphrey, the most vocal liberal in the Senate during the 1950s. On the right is Dick Russell, the leading conservative, whom Lyndon called "the best friend I've got" in the Senate. Lyndon believed that there are three sides to an issue, the third side being the one that brings the other two sides together for a compromise. He said often to two opposing sides, "Let's reason together."

congressmen and senators to make a majority in both the House and the Senate. Sam Rayburn was again the House Speaker. Illinois Senator Scott Lucas was elected by the Democrats to be the Senate Majority Leader.

But Lyndon knew who really ran the Senate—Dick Russell. Because of his seniority, Russell decided who got on what committees. If a young senator wanted to be on a committee where he would get a lot of attention, he had to get along with Dick Russell.

Lyndon, bringing his kids each week to see a childless Dick Russell who loved kids, got along with a new "daddy."

He also got along with liberals, such as Hubert Humphrey, who was demanding loudly that the Senate pass laws to guarantee blacks their civil rights. Southerners glared at Humphrey because they opposed those laws. Lyndon, however, chatted amiably with Hubert.

Lyndon also struck up a friendship with a twenty-one-year-old Senate page (a messenger boy). Soon Lyndon was inviting the short, stubby Bobby Baker to his office. Bobby Baker had been a page for seven years. He knew what each senator was really like—which ones worked hard and which ones were lazy, which ones drank too much and which ones were greedy for power or money.

"Lyndon and I," Baker once said, "became very close very quickly. . . . He was very quick to learn all there was to know about each and every senator." Soon other senators, seeing them together so often, called Baker "Little Lyndon."

The junior senator from Texas moved his family into a two-story white brick colonial house near Washington's Cleveland Park section. Harry Truman had lived there, and FBI chief J. Edgar Hoover was a neighbor.

Next door lived Dr. and Mrs. Ollie Reed. When the Johnson girls scampered home from school, they often beelined to the Reeds. Usually their parents were not home. Lady Bird had to fly often to Austin to oversee her Texas Broadcasting Corporation, which now owned both KTBC radio and a TV station, the only channel in Austin. From dawn to night, Lyndon roamed the corridors, cloak-room, offices, and floor of the Senate.

The girls watched goldfish dart about in a small pond in the Reeds' backyard. They played with Dr. and Mrs. Reed. Years later Dr. Reed said to Lyndon, "Your daughter Lynda is lovely." Lyndon said, "She should look lovely. After all, you raised her."

A frequent visitor from Texas was Rebekah Johnson, Lyndon's mother. She told the fascinated girls true stories of how their great-grandfather and grandfather had driven cattle to Kansas on the old Chisholm Trail.

By 1950 the Johnsons were millionaires. Profits poured into Texas Broadcasting. Some people in Austin complained, "Why do we have only one TV channel?" They asked whether the Federal Communications Commission was giving the Johnsons an illegal break by allowing only one TV station. The FCC replied that other cities the size of Austin—Topeka, Kansas, for example—had only one channel. And anyway, said the FCC, the Johnsons never asked that Austin have only one channel. Moreover, no one had ever applied to start a second TV station.

With their radio-TV profits, Lyndon and Lady Bird bought back the 433-acre ranch along the Perdinales that Lyndon's grandfather had owned and his father had lost on his cotton gamble. The musty old ranch buildings were swept and painted. Lyndon stocked the ponds with fish. He bought cattle and horses.

The ranch was small as Texas spreads go. Sam Rayburn called it a "little old farm." But Lyndon and Lady Bird liked to stroll its grassy slopes. To Lynda and Luci, the LBJ Ranch, as Lyndon dubbed it, was a peaceful oasis where the Johnsons could escape the heat and bustle of Washington. As Lady Bird put it, the LBJ Ranch became "our heart's home."

By 1950 Harry Truman and the Democrats had lost much of the public support they'd had in 1948. Truman had sent American troops to South Korea to stop a wave of invaders from Communist North Korea. The Americans lost many bloody battles. The public blamed Truman. At home, strikes paralyzed several industries and prices soared. Again, Americans blamed Truman.

Truman had asked Scott Lucas to steer his Fair Deal bills through the Senate. One was a civil-rights bill giving blacks the same rights to vote as whites. Southerners argued against the civil-rights bills. That bill, and many other Truman Fair Deal bills, were defeated by a solid bloc of Republican and Democratic conservatives. Lyndon stood nearly always among them.

Lyndon welcomes visitors to the LBJ Ranch while mounted on one of his horses. He told visitors hair-raising stories of how his grandfather and great-grandfathers – the Johnsons and the Buntons – fought raiding Indians from a fort in nearby Johnson City.

In the 1950 elections, many Democrats lost. Among those defeated was Scott Lucas. Seeing what had happened to Lucas, no Democratic senator was anxious to be Majority Leader. Dick Russell finally persuaded Arizona Senator Ernie McFarland to take the job. McFarland needed an assistant leader (called the Whip).

Lyndon offered to be the Whip, a job no one else wanted. As the Whip, he would be more than a freshman senator. He would get headlines, and Texans could be proud of him. Lyndon knew he had to run again in 1954. He had not forgotten how he had won by only 87 votes in 1948.

He was lucky he didn't have to run in 1952.

"We want Ike! We want Ike!" chanted millions of Americans in 1952. They wanted their new president to be Dwight David Eisenhower, the World War II hero/general known as Ike. Ike, a Republican, won easily, capturing several southern states, including Texas. He brought with him to Washington almost a hundred Republican senators and representatives. Among the Democrats buried under Ike's landslide was Ernie McFarland.

The Democrats needed a Minority Leader, but few Democratic senators wanted to stand up to oppose the bills of the popular Ike.

Lyndon wanted the job to get the attention he knew he would need for 1954. Senate liberals, led by Hubert Humphrey, said he was too conservative. The liberals proposed Idaho's Jim Murray.

Lyndon, who loved to use the phone and sometimes made as many as twenty calls an hour, called Hubert and asked, "How are you going to vote?"

"I can't vote for you."

"Well, I'm sorry. You know I'm going to win. . . . Who do you think is going to vote for Murray?"

Humphrey ticked off names. After each name, Lyndon stopped him and said, "He isn't going to vote for Murray. . . . He isn't. . . . He isn't . . . "

Humphrey said Lyndon was wrong. The next day the Democrats voted. "I'll never forget it," Humphrey said years later. "He was just as right as day. They voted for Johnson."

Lyndon had known how they would vote because Bobby Baker, who knew the mind of every senator, had told him how they would vote.

The new Minority Leader called Hubert to his office. "Now let me tell you something," Lyndon said. "I know we don't agree on a number of things, but at least we can get along...." Lyndon told Humphrey that he would put Jim Murray on the important Policy Committee. After a victory in politics, Lyndon knew, you put out your hand and helped up your fallen foe. The next time he or she might be grateful enough to join your side.

As the new Minority Leader, Lyndon had an idea. It concerned the Senate seniority system, which was precious to older senators. Men, such as Dick Russell, who had been senators for twenty years or more, sat on all the important committees. New senators were sidelined onto committees that got no attention.

Why not, Lyndon whispered to the frozen-faced Dick Russell, make a *slight*—Lyndon emphasized "slight"— change in the seniority system? Every senator, even junior ones, would be placed on at least one big committee.

Russell liked the idea. He thought that new senators should get a brief stay in the spotlight so they could learn.

Lyndon went around to new Senators, such as Massachusetts's John F. Kennedy, and put them on one or two big committees. Each now owed *him* a favor. (Of Kennedy, Lyndon said to Bobby Baker, "He's a nice kid and probably has some future.")

13

The Johnson Treatment

Senator Homer Capehart, a big grin on his plump face, strolled across the Senate floor. He stopped at the desk of the Majority Leader. He stared down at Lyndon and said, "Lyndon, this is one time I've really got you."

Lyndon nodded, a weak grin on his face.

In January 1955, when the Congress gathered, the Democrats had more Senators, by one, than the Republicans, because of the 1954 elections. (Lyndon had been reelected easily.) Lyndon was now the Majority Leader. At forty-seven, he was the youngest ever.

Until now he had not tried to unite Democrats against Ike's bills. Ike had too many Republican votes in the Congress, for one thing. For another, Ike was too popular. Democrats would only make enemies among voters by trying to stop Ike's bills.

But now Lyndon had a slim majority in the Senate. He tried to squeeze the Democrats' bills through the Senate. Lyndon and other Democrats knew that Eisenhower would probably be reelected in 1956. But they might be able to capture the presidency in 1960, because a new law had been passed declaring that a president could serve for only two terms. To win, the Democrats knew they had to

Lyndon has a smile for President Eisenhower during a ceremony. During the 1950s, Lyndon, Eisenhower, and Sam Rayburn were the three most powerful men in Washington. The Eisenhower years, perhaps because those three got along so well, were among the most peaceful in American history.

capture the votes in the big cities. Cities were filled with workers and blacks, who usually voted for the Democrats but who had swung to Ike.

To win back those voters, the Democrats had to offer them help. That meant, for one thing, cheap public housing — and lots of it. The Democrats proposed a bill to give public housing to 135,000 families. Republicans and southern Democrats opposed the bill.

Republican Homer Capehart offered an amendment to the bill. Capehart's amendment reduced the number of housing units to 35,000.

The shrewd Capehart figured that southern Democrats would join with Republicans to vote for his amendment. Only 35,000 public-housing units was easier to swallow than 135,000. Liberal Democrats would vote for it too — they didn't want to be recorded as being *against* public housing. But only 35,000 units would not help the Democrats in 1960.

Capehart glowed with amusement. He had trapped Lyndon. The vote was set for the next day. That evening Lyndon began to apply to this problem what other senators called the Johnson Treatment.

"When Johnson wanted to persuade you of something," a senator once said, " ... you really felt as if a Saint Bernard dog had licked your face for an hour and pawed you all over.... "

"When he talked to someone," another said, "Johnson used to get up right close and poke him in the chest. At the same time he would drop his head and cock it to one side, and really come in to talk to you with his head coming in under your face. And he would poke you in the chest with his finger and cock his head and talk, all at the same time."

Applying the Johnson Treatment, Lyndon told southern conservatives, "Isn't a little public housing of 35,000 units the same as big public housing of 135,000?" At least, he pointed out, as far as their supporters saw it. "You vote for even a little public housing," he said, "and people back home are going to be sore at you."

Southern conservatives said he was right. The next day, as each southern vote was counted against the Capehart amendment, "Capehart's chin almost bounced off his desk," a reporter wrote. The amendment was easily defeated.

Lyndon now gave the Johnson Treatment to big-city Republicans and Democrats who had voted for the amendment. If you voted for 35,000 units, he said, you've got to vote for 135,000, or people back home will say you don't really believe in public housing. The bill passed the Senate easily, 65–25.

At the same time, Lyndon was building the Johnson Network. This network was made up of senators whom he could count on to vote the way he wanted whenever he badly needed their votes. A lot of them were young senators, such as Jack Kennedy, who owed him favors. "People of your state don't care how you vote on this bill one way or the other," he told them. "But the Leader cares, it means a lot to me." And he would add, "The first thing you ought to learn in Congress is that you get along by going along."

Once, a young senator, Idaho's Frank Church, listened to that advice but then voted against Lyndon. "For the next six months," Church said, "he never spoke to me. . . . He just simply ignored me." Then Church came through with a vote that got a Johnson bill passed by the Senate. "Lyndon was warmly and assertively grateful," Church said. "He would just pick you up and squeeze all the air out of you. All at once I was in the Garden of Eden and Lyndon Johnson could not be lavish enough." Church and his wife were soon flying off on a government-paid tour of South America.

Lyndon knew what each senator wanted in return for his vote. Bobby Baker would tell him. "If he asked Senator

Harry Byrd to ... vote a certain way," Arkansas Senator William Fulbright once said, "he always knew what it was that Harry wanted in return."

Lyndon ran the Johnson Network from behind his large desk in the Senate office building. There were as many as three or four phones on that desk. A cigarette dangled from his lips, one of fifty to sixty he puffed furiously each day. He often ate at the desk, wolfing down a cold frankfurter or hamburger. From early morning to nearly midnight on days when the Senate was voting, he dashed from office to office to apply the Johnson Treatment to Senators on his expanding Johnson Network.

Lady Bird and his daughters seldom saw him from Monday to Saturday. Late at night he sat with Sam Rayburn and other leaders, talking politics and sipping whiskey. His weight had soared to 225 pounds. Sam glanced at him with anxious eyes. He warned Lyndon to slow down.

Lyndon could not. There was too much to do. On Saturday, July 2, 1955, he was too busy to attend Luci's eighth birthday party. He held a press conference and roared angrily at a reporter who asked a question he didn't like.

He jumped, still angry, into a limousine to be driven to the Virginia country estate of Herman Brown, the Texas multimillionaire builder. On the way, Lyndon felt ill. His chest began to hurt. It felt, he said, "as though there was two hundred pounds on it." He thought he had indigestion.

At Brown's mansion he stretched out on a bed. Another guest, Senator Clinton Anderson, put his finger on Lyndon's pulse. He felt his heartbeat.

"Lyndon," Anderson said, "you're having a heart attack!"

14

The Great Compromiser

For weeks Lyndon had to lie quietly in the hospital. When he went home to the LBJ Ranch, doctors told him he had to eat and drink less, stop smoking, and lose weight, or else another heart attack would kill him.

Lady Bird ordered a pool built near the main house of the ranch. Each day Lyndon splashed up and down the pool. His daughters swam with him. For the first time, the two girls, now eleven and eight, felt close to a father who had always been on the run.

Returning to Washington early in 1956, he looked a different man. Once paunchy, he was now gaunt, the weight on his six-foot-four frame down from 230 to 180 pounds. He was keeping his promise not to smoke. He sipped one drink a day. He ate leisurely, nutritious lunches. He came home at five, napped, exercised, and went to bed early.

He was still the Majority Leader, one of the five or six best-known Democrats in the nation. Later that summer the Democrats would pick a nominee to run against Eisenhower. Lyndon knew the nominee wouldn't be himself. "I've got two strikes against me," he told a friend. "I'm from the South and I've just had a heart attack. People will wonder if they should vote for a president who might be dead tomorrow."

The Johnson daughters had attended public schools in Washington and Austin. They now attended the National Cathedral School for Girls. The school, operated by the Episcopal church, gave religious training. Lady Bird had received that training, and she wanted it for her girls.

By now the Johnson radio-TV station and ranch were worth close to $10 million. But Lyndon kept an anxious eye on bills. When he came home and saw a bulb lit when it wasn't necessary, he snapped at his brother, who sometimes stayed with them, "What are you trying to do, Sam Houston, keep the electric company in business?" He snapped off the light, a money-saving habit he would never lose even as the most powerful man in the free world.

In 1956 the Republicans again nominated Eisenhower and Richard Nixon. The Democrats chose Adlai Stevenson, who had been their nominee in 1952 as well, and Estes Kefauver as his running mate. The surprise of the convention was John F. Kennedy, the handsome Massachusetts senator, who came close to winning the nomination for vice president.

Ike and Nixon won easily. When Congress met in January 1957, the three most powerful political leaders in the nation were President Eisenhower, Speaker Rayburn, and Majority Leader Johnson. All three had been born in Texas (though Ike grew up in Kansas). "We Texans have got to stick together," Ike often told Rayburn and Lyndon.

Ike wanted a civil-rights law passed. It would give blacks the same rights as whites to enter public places. No longer would blacks have to sit in the backs of buses. They could eat in restaurants that had proclaimed *For Whites Only.*

They could line up outside a polling booth and vote side by side with whites.

Black people, Ike and Lyndon both realized, could not be held down much longer as second-class citizens. A 1954 Supreme Court decision had already ordered that black children and white children would be allowed to sit side by side in school. There could be no more all-white and all-black schools.

Black people believed their time for equality had come. In the North and South, they were marching, sometimes peacefully and sometimes angrily, for their rights. Both Ike and Lyndon knew that the party that got the credit for passing civil-rights laws would win the votes of millions of black voters in future elections. Lyndon had a plan.

When Ike sent his civil-rights bill to Congress, Lyndon told Texas voters that he would vote against it. That pleased some white Texans who were against *any* equality bill.

Then, quietly, he began to concoct a Democratic civil-rights bill. He talked to southern senators. "A civil-rights bill is going to be passed. Do you want a strong one that Humphrey and his liberals will write? Or do you want a weak one that we will write?"

He talked to the liberals. "You've been trying for ten years to get a rights bill passed. What have you got so far? Nothing. I will get you something. Half a loaf is a lot better to a hungry man than no loaf at all."

Ike's bill had four parts. Lyndon knew that Parts II and IV would be fought tooth and nail by southerners. Those parts ordered tough enforcement and penalties when civil rights were violated. Lyndon persuaded the Johnson Network to vote for his bill, which erased Part II and softened Part IV.

The weakened bill passed Congress. It went to the White House for Ike's signature, needed to make it law. Ike said angrily that a Republican bill had become Lyndon's Democratic bill.

Vice President Nixon told friends he would ask Ike to

veto the bill. Lyndon, riding in his limousine, got a call on one of his favorite gadgets—the car phone. Nixon was on his way to the White House.

Hastily, Lyndon dialed the number of Republican Minority Leader Bill Knowland. He asked Knowland how it would look to black people if a Republican president vetoed a civil-rights bill.

Knowland got to Ike's side before Nixon. Ike signed the bill. In the South, Lyndon got the credit for weakening the law. In the North and the West, he got credit for making into law a bill that was, "after all," wrote a *New York Times* reporter, "with all its shortcomings, the first genuine civil-rights measure" since the Civil War.

He had made friends among liberal and conservative Democrats. But as 1960 came nearer, he told friends that he still had "the smell of magnolia" on him—the perfume of the South that would make Democratic delegates draw away from him.

From Washington, in the spring of 1960, he watched Hubert Humphrey and Jack Kennedy battle to collect Democratic delegates. He told Bobby Baker, "Every night I go to bed, and I never know if I'm going to wake up alive the next morning. I'm just not physically capable of running for the presidency."

Yet he hoped the delegates would come to the convention in Los Angeles divided between Kennedy and Humphrey. Then they might pick him—the Great Compromiser. "That," said one of his aides, Bill Moyer, "is how he saw himself."

He announced that he would be a candidate. When he came to Los Angeles with Lady Bird and his two daughters, who were now teenagers, hot words began to fly between the Kennedy and Johnson camps. Lyndon called Jack Kennedy and his younger brother, Bobby (his campaign manager), "two spoiled brats" who were buying delegates with their rich father's millions.

Lyndon dared Kennedy to debate him in front of the Texas delegation. Kennedy showed up. He told the delegates that Lyndon was such a great senator he ought to stay in the Senate. Lyndon smiled faintly, aware that he had been outwitted.

The delegates began to vote two nights later. Lyndon got the Texas votes, but few others. Kennedy was nominated on the first ballot.

L.B.J. watched his TV set as the delegates chanted, "Kennedy! Kennedy!" He clicked off the set. "Well," he said, "that's it." He talked about taking his daughters to Disneyland the next day.

But Democrats were whispering Lyndon's name into the ears of Jack and Bobby Kennedy.

15

Mr. Vice President

The phone rang in the darkened bedroom. Still half-asleep, Lady Bird picked up the receiver. Lyndon slept soundly. It was the morning after Kennedy's nomination. "Yes, please hold on," she said into the phone. She awakened her husband. "It's Jack Kennedy, and he wants to speak to you."

Lyndon, blinking, took the phone. He agreed to meet with Kennedy later that morning.

Rumors were spreading across Los Angeles: Kennedy wanted Johnson as his vice president. Lyndon could bring in southern states, where Kennedy was disliked because he was liberal and Catholic.

Labor leaders told Kennedy he couldn't pick Johnson. They recalled his vote for the Taft-Hartley bill and distrusted him. So did most black leaders, because he was a Southerner and because they knew how he had weakened the civil-rights bill.

For hours that morning, Kennedy and his advisers, including his brother Bobby, debated. Lyndon would cost them votes in northern states. But the Democrats could probably win those states themselves, even with Lyndon as a running mate. Kennedy seemed to make up his mind. He went to Lyndon's hotel room and asked him to run. Lyndon said he would consider the offer.

Sam Rayburn had told Lyndon not to run with Kennedy. Then a friend said to Sam, "Do you want Nixon to be president?" Sam agreed: The Democrats would lose to Richard Nixon, the Republican nominee, if Lyndon wasn't on the ticket. Sam told Lyndon to accept Kennedy's offer.

But now, back in his room, Kennedy wavered. His aides were telling him that many blacks and union workers would desert the Democratic ranks rather than vote for Lyndon.

Finally, Jack told his brother Bobby to go to Lyndon's room and tell him that the offer of the vice presidency had to be withdrawn—there was too much opposition.

Bobby left to deliver the message. Jack was then told that only Lyndon could guarantee victory in Texas and other southern states. The Democrats had to carry those states or they would lose.

Kennedy made his final decision: It would be Lyndon. He phoned Lyndon.

"Do you really want me?" Lyndon asked.

"Yes, I do."

"Well, if you really want me, I'll do it."

Minutes later Bobby came into Lyndon's room. He said that Kennedy didn't want Johnson on the ticket.

Stunned and angry, Lyndon glared at Bobby. Sam Rayburn, who was standing nearby, shouted for someone to call Kennedy.

The call got through to Kennedy, who said, "Bobby's out of date. I've already announced that Johnson is the candidate." He asked to speak to Lyndon and again assured him that he was the man he wanted.

"All right," Lyndon muttered. He walked by Bobby Kennedy, believing Bobby had not wanted him on the ticket.

Lynda Bird Johnson had thought the convention was over for her father after Kennedy was nominated. She had gone to Disneyland. There, watching fireworks, she heard a waitress say that the convention had just nominated Lyndon for vice president.

Bobby Kennedy whispers to Lyndon shortly after Lyndon accepted John Kennedy's offer to be the nominee for vice president at the 1960 convention. Lyndon's narrow eyes reflect the suspicion he always harbored toward Bobby Kennedy.

Lynda hurried back to the hotel. She walked, red-eared, into her father's room. Lyndon fixed her with a steely glare. He had forgotten all about the talk of going to Disneyland. "What do you think we came here for," he growled, "Disneyland?"

Kennedy and Johnson won—by a whisker. They beat Nixon and his running mate, Henry Cabot Lodge, by the fewest number of votes in any presidential election until then. Texas, which had been lost to the Republicans in 1952 and 1956, voted for Kennedy, as did three other southern states. Without those states, Kennedy would likely have lost. The final decision to put Lyndon on the ticket had proved to be right.

President Kennedy listens attentively to his vice president as he talks to reporters shortly after they were elected. The president always tried to put Lyndon up front, at his side, when they were in public together.

As the vice president, Lyndon presided over the Senate. He had no real power. He only voted when there was a tie, and that didn't happen often.

Not much happens to vice presidents—they don't get much publicity. "The job," Cactus Jack Garner once said, "is not worth a pitcher of warm spit." A Washington joke told of the mother whose one son went to sea while the other became vice president. "Neither," the joke went, "was ever heard from again."

A year earlier Lyndon had been one of the nation's three most powerful political leaders. Now he was an invisible man.

But President Kennedy didn't want his vice president to vanish into the shadows. Whenever he traveled with

Lyndon, he turned to aides and shouted, "Where's Lyndon?" The aides escorted Lyndon forward to stand, grinning, next to Kennedy as they waved at crowds.

Kennedy promised Americans that the U.S. would rocket a spaceship to the moon in the 1960s. He made Lyndon the head of the space agency.

Lyndon, however, was still sure that Bobby Kennedy did not like him. He heard how White House people called him "Old Uncle Corn Pone" and imitated his southern drawl. He believed Bobby had made up the name.

Lyndon wanted a Texan, Sarah T. Hughes, appointed a U.S. Judge. Bobby, who was Kennedy's attorney general, had to approve the appointment. Bobby said that the sixty-four-year-old Hughes was too old. Lyndon asked Bobby to change his mind, but Bobby said no.

Bobby met Speaker Sam Rayburn a few days later and asked why one of President Kennedy's bills was stuck in the House. Sam said, "That bill of yours will pass as soon as Sarah Hughes becomes a federal judge."

Bobby protested that she was too old. "Sonny," said the hard-bitten Sam to the thirty-five-year-old Bobby, "everybody seems old to you."

Bobby laughed. He approved the nomination of Sarah Hughes.

Lyndon was angry when he heard. He knew that Texas politicians would say that Sam Rayburn could get an appointment through the White House—and the vice president couldn't. He was sure Bobby wanted to destroy him.

Meanwhile, though, the vice president's wife was happy. She and Lyndon bought a three-story mansion in Washington. They called it The Elms. Almost every weekend they stood at the gates to welcome guests—movie stars, foreign ambassadors, senators, and Supreme Court justices—to glittering parties.

"I had a ball when he became vice president," Lady Bird later said. "We entertained and we traveled a lot, the things

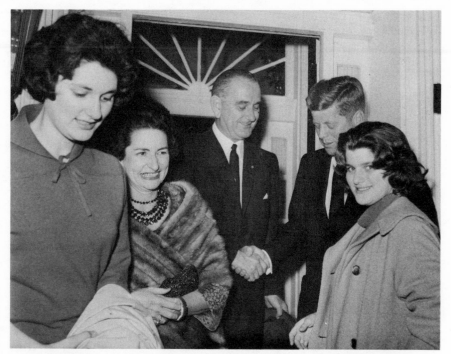

The Johnson family says good-bye to President Kennedy after having dinner with the Kennedys. Lynda Bird stands next to her mother; Luci is on the right with an impish glint in her eyes. She was thirteen, her sister sixteen. Lady Bird later called her years as the wife of the vice president the happiest of her many years in Washington.

I had done very little of before. But it was a life that was not nearly as pleasant for him as it was for me."

At meetings in the White House, Lyndon looked sullen and said little. Kennedy aides said that the vice president did not want to make decisions that might backfire into his face. He wanted no scars on him, they said, because he wanted to run for president in 1968, when Kennedy would have to retire.

To give Lyndon more attention and importance, Kennedy sent him on goodwill trips to Asia. He went to Vietnam,

where a Communist guerrilla chief, Ho Chi Minh, was
battling the troops of South Vietnam. Returning to Washington, Lyndon told Kennedy that the U.S. had to help the
South Vietnamese with money and weapons. President
Kennedy agreed. By 1962 a handful of Americans were
showing the Vietnamese how to use modern American
weapons.

Coming back from one overseas trip in 1962, Lyndon
was met at the airport by a haggard Sam Rayburn. Mr.
Sam was dying. He told Lyndon he was going home.

Sam went back to Texas. Every weekend Lyndon flew
from Washington to sit at his bedside. When Sam died,
Lyndon came back to Washington even more quiet and
depressed—until he was jarred into fury by a scandal.

By 1963 Bobby Baker knew all about the private lives of
every senator. He was so powerful that he was called the
101st senator. Then a senator learned that Baker was
part-owner of a company that put vending machines into
factories that had contracts with the government. For a
Senate employee, that was illegal. Baker had to quit his
Senate job.

Reporters wrote stories telling the public how close
"Little Lyndon" had been to the vice president. Lyndon
roared to reporters that he hardly knew Baker—while
senators chuckled. To his aides, Lyndon snarled that Attorney General Bobby Kennedy had put detectives on Baker's
trail to embarrass the vice president.

During the summer of 1963, Lyndon heard talk of a
"Dump Lyndon" movement within the White House. President Kennedy told reporters he wanted Lyndon on the
ticket as vice president in 1964. But Lyndon still brooded,
sure that Bobby was trying to talk his brother into pick-
ing someone else.

"I wish to hell you'd persuade Kennedy not to come." A
Dallas businessman was speaking to Lyndon late in
November 1963. Lyndon nodded. He knew that "hate
groups" had hinted that the president, a liberal and a

Catholic, might be killed if he visited Dallas. Lyndon told the businessman that Kennedy was determined to go to Dallas.

The Texas Democrats were quarrelling among themselves. Kennedy hoped that when the feuding Democrats heard thousands cheer for him in Dallas, they would want to unite behind a winner.

Lyndon chatted with Kennedy at a reception in Houston on the morning of November 22. A warm drizzle was drying up as the sun edged from behind the clouds. Lyndon told Kennedy that his youngest sister, Lucia, wanted to meet the president. Kennedy suggested that Lyndon bring his sister to his suite after the reception.

As Lyndon and Lucia came into the room, Kennedy was changing his shirt. He shook hands with Lucia. Lyndon remarked that Dallas would give the president a grand reception. Kennedy grinned and said, "You can be sure of two things"—pronouncing *sure* with his Harvard accent as *shu-ah*—"we're going to carry two states next year, Massachusetts and Texas."

Lyndon laughed. "We're going to carry a lot more than those two."

They would never speak together again. Lyndon left to board a plane. It flew to Dallas ahead of Air Force One, which carried a president to the cheers of hundreds of thousands and the rifle of one.

16

Mr. President

A little more than an hour after John Kennedy's assassination, Lyndon walked into the cabin of Air Force One and heard Walter Cronkite tell the nation that Lyndon Johnson was president of the United States. If there was an army of snipers trying to gun down the nation's leaders, Lyndon told Kennedy's aides, he should be sworn in immediately as president so he could take charge of the government.

An aide called the attorney general, who was in Washington. Lyndon took the phone and talked to Bobby, who had just learned that his brother was dead. Bobby's voice was composed. He said Lyndon was correct—he should be sworn in immediately.

Lyndon asked that Sarah T. Hughes, the recently appointed federal judge, be brought to Air Force One. Jackie Kennedy, meanwhile, had arrived with the coffin of her husband. She sat next to it in a rear cabin.

Lyndon invited her to come to his cabin for the swearing-in. She arrived, looking stunned. Lyndon and Lady Bird stared with tears in their eyes. Jackie's pink suit was spattered with her husband's dried blood. Lady Bird offered to help her change into other clothes, but she refused. She stood next to Lyndon as Judge Hughes administered the oath that made Lyndon Baines Johnson the thirty-sixth president of the United States.

Aboard Air Force One in Dallas, Lyndon is sworn in as president, Lady Bird on the left, a stunned Jackie Kennedy on the right. Judge Sarah Hughes holds the Bible as Lyndon swears on it to uphold the Constitution of the United States as its thirty-sixth president.

Shortly after Air Force One landed in Washington, Lyndon wrote to John Kennedy's small children, Caroline and John. To the younger, John, he wrote, "It will be many years before you fully understand what a great man your father was. His loss is a deep personal tragedy for all of us. But I wanted you particularly to know they share your grief. You can always be proud of him. Affectionately, Lyndon Johnson."

A few days later, his two teenagers sat in the balcony above the House as their father spoke to Congress. Lynda and Luci had learned overnight what it was like to be the children of a president. Secret Service bodyguards walked at their side wherever they went. Their friends in school had to stare at them from a distance.

To a hushed Congress and millions of still-grieving Americans watching him on TV, Lyndon began, "All I have I would have given gladly not to be standing here today." He reminded his listeners that President Kennedy had said, "Let us begin" the work of making the nation better. Now, he said, "let us continue" that work.

In that speech, and to other people during the next few weeks, he explained how he wanted that work to continue in three areas: 1) new and stronger civil-rights laws; 2) laws that would help people to get the training and other help they needed to lift them out of poverty; 3) the defense of South Vietnam against the attacks by Ho Chi Minh.

Hubert Humphrey was appearing on a TV show, "Face the Nation." Reporters quizzed him about a tough civil-rights bill that President Johnson had sent to Congress. Did Humphrey think that the Senate Republican leader, Everett Dirksen, would support the bill?

Humphrey said that Senator Dirksen was a great American. "And he is going to see the necessity of this legislation. I predict that before this bill is through, Senator Dirksen will be its champion."

A few minutes later the show ended. Humphrey was handed a telephone. The president was on the line.

"Boy, that was right," Lyndon shouted. "You just keep at that. Don't let those bomb throwers"—Lyndon meant other liberals—"talk you out of seeing Dirksen. You go in there to see Dirksen. You drink with Dirksen. You talk to Dirksen. You listen to Dirksen."

Lyndon knew that liberal Democrats and liberal Republicans would vote for the bill. He knew southern Democrats and southern Republicans would vote against it. The deciding votes would come from conservative northern Republicans, whose lead man was Dirksen.

The president gives to black leader Dr. Martin Luther King, Jr., the pen he used to sign the 1964 civil-rights law. Later, Dr. King and others asked the president for another law to outlaw the poll tax.

Following Lyndon's advice, Humphrey cornered Dirksen each morning in the Senate cloakroom. "Everett," the bouncy Humphrey shouted, "we can't pass this bill without you. With you in the lead, Everett, this bill will pass. It will go down in history, Everett." Later Humphrey said to friends, "That meant, of course, that *he* would go down in history, which interested him a great deal."

The bill passed, 73–27. Lyndon signed the bill, which had been written by President Kennedy, into law. Black leaders told Lyndon that the Kennedy law would not help blacks to vote in states which made people pay a tax to vote. Poor blacks could not afford to pay the poll tax. Lyndon promised to write a civil-rights bill that would outlaw the poll tax.

"The whole idea of declaring a big war on poverty and ending it for all time . . . appealed to him very much," said a friend of the new president. The Hill Country boy who had worked on a road gang for two dollars a day had never forgotten how frightening poverty could be. Early in 1964 he told Congress, "This administration here and now declares unconditional war on poverty in America."

He sent to Congress a bill that would create a billion-dollar project overseen by an Office of Economic Opportunity. Most Democrats, both conservative and liberal, wanted to support the new president. So did some Republicans, especially liberals. The bill, and others like it, sailed through Congress, and Lyndon signed them into law.

The Job Corps began to train poor people to take better-paying jobs. The Head Start program taught poor preschool children to read and write before the first grade. By 1965 almost two million Americans were studying and training in programs run by the Office of Economic Opportunity.

"Let us continue" to make America better, Lyndon had told the nation. Now he had a name for that new America. In a speech to the graduating class at the University of Michigan on May 22, 1964, Lyndon said, "In your time we have the opportunity to move not only toward the rich society and the powerful society, but upward to the Great Society."

The Great Society. In the Great Society there would be no second-class people who were looked down upon because of their color or religion. There would be no poor and hungry.

Lyndon studied the plans for his Great Society. He would need new laws for it, but he knew how to get Congress to pass new laws.

But while Lyndon studied those plans, generals and admirals plucked at his sleeve. Reluctantly, Lyndon turned to look over his shoulder at a war in Vietnam that had become bloodier and bloodier.

How could he squash Ho Chi Minh and turn back to his Great Society?

17

"As a Barefoot Boy..."

Democrats streamed into Atlantic City for their 1964 convention. Almost everyone knew Lyndon Johnson would be picked to run for president in the fall of 1964—everyone, that is, except Lyndon Johnson.

He had told the family cook the day before the convention opened that he would soon be "coming out of the White House." He wrote a letter to the American people saying that he would not run but would "go back home as I've wanted to since the day I took this job."

He had strutted, swaggered, and blustered through his life. But at times he had stopped short, nervous and uncertain. In 1936 he had worried that he might not be good enough to be the Texas NYA director. "Lyndon was not the supremely confident person he seemed," Lady Bird had said then. In his campaigns, he had sometimes stopped, depressed, sure he would lose.

Now he wondered: Am I tough enough to hurl young men to their death in Vietnamese battles? And could I lead a people whose college youth were beginning to shout, "Get out of Vietnam!"

Lyndon told his press secretary that he didn't think he "could lead all of America." The press secretary said gently, "Do you think Barry Goldwater can lead all the people?"

Lady Bird shows in her eyes both the laughter everyone enjoyed when they heard Lyndon tell a story of the Hill Country, and the love she had for a husband of more than thirty years. They are in the president's cabin on Air Force One flying back to Washington after a vacation on the ranch.

The feisty, rich Goldwater, an Arizona senator, had been picked by the Republicans to run for president. He demanded that America destroy Ho Chi Minh and his peasant army with more bombers. He declared that Lyndon's spending for his Great Society was taking too much money out of the wallets and purses of taxpayers.

Lady Bird heard that Lyndon was hesitating. Rarely did she argue with her husband. "She tiptoed around the big moose when he was roaring," Hubert Humphrey once said. "She stroked him and said, 'Now, dear,' until he calmed down."

She stroked Lyndon with a letter. She knew that if she talked to him about it, "he would probably interrupt me and outtalk me." So she wrote:

Beloved—You are as brave a man as Harry Truman or F.D.R. or Lincoln. . . . You have been strong, patient, determined beyond any words of mine to express. I honor you for it. So does most of the country.

To step out now would be *wrong* for your country and I can see nothing but a lonely wasteland for your future. Your friends would be frozen in embarrassed silence and your enemies jeering. . . .

In the final analysis I can't carry any of the burden you talked of—so I know it's only your choice. But I know you are as brave as any of the thirty-five [former presidents]. I love you always. Bird.

The next day Lyndon flew to Atlantic City to accept the nomination for president.

Flying with him was a smiling Hubert Humphrey. After waiting until the last moment, while Hubert sweated with worry, Lyndon announced that his old liberal ally, Hubert, would run with him as vice president.

First, though, Lyndon called in Bobby Kennedy, who was still the attorney general. He knew that Kennedy wanted to be vice president. He told the nervous Kennedy that he would not pick him. Later, gleefully, Lyndon told his aides that Bobby's face "changed and he started to swallow. He looked sick. His Adam's apple bounced up and down like a yo-yo."

As he had done to the Black Stars who spurned him, Lyndon had taken his revenge on another man he thought had tried to shut a door in his face.

In the campaign, the Democrats branded Goldwater the "war candidate." His bombings, they said, might set the world ablaze in a nuclear holocaust. And he had voted, they pointed out, against help for the poor and against civil rights for blacks.

On the final day of the campaign, Lyndon went back to Austin and the Hill Country for his last speech ever as a candidate. He stood in front of the Texas House of Repre-

A triumphant Lyndon shakes hands with a dour Bobby
Kennedy whose eyes show his mistrust for Lyndon. In 1964
Lyndon told Kennedy he was not wanted as Lyndon's vice
president. Behind the two is Adlai Stevenson, the Democrats'
nominee for President in 1952 and 1956 (he lost both times
to Ike). In Lyndon's lapel is the Silver Star ribbon he wore all
his life.

sentatives and said, "It was here as a barefoot boy around my father's desk ... that I first learned that government is not an enemy of the people. It is the people. I learned here that poverty and ignorance are only the basic weaknesses of a free society, and that both of them are bad habits and can be stopped."

Lyndon swamped Goldwater, winning by 15 million votes, the biggest lead in any presidential election until then. And he carried on his coattails so many Democrat lawmakers that they were the majority in both the House and Senate.

After the election, Lyndon relaxed at the ranch. Though only fifty-six, young for a president, he spoke wishfully of retiring. He wanted to stare across the Hill Country at the sunsets—"the greatest thing you ever saw," he told visitors.

But first he had to finish the building of his Great Society. He had to get the laws he needed passed in the first two years of his term, he said. A president started a new term with lots of "money" to spend. By "money," Lyndon meant the favors he could give congressmen—jobs for the people of their districts, for example. By "money," he also meant the favors he could collect from lawmakers he had pulled into Washington on his coattails. The president could spend that "money" to "buy" votes so that Congress passed his bills into law.

The trouble is that, just like a shopper in a supermarket, presidents spend until their purses are empty. Without those favors, Lyndon said, suddenly depressed, "something is going to come up, either something like the Vietnam War or something else, where I will begin to lose all I have now."

In the South, meanwhile, a black leader, Dr. Martin Luther King, Jr., led marchers demanding the end of the poll tax so that more blacks could vote. The marchers sang, "We Shall Overcome!" which was Dr. King's rallying cry. Marching into Selma, Alabama, Dr. King's followers were beaten by police with clubs and electric prods.

Lyndon watched the brutal beatings on TV—each night he watched all three TV news shows. He was horrified. Like many southerners and northerners, he had once thought that the races should be kept separate but equal. Like many Americans in the 1960s, he had changed his mind and now thought there should be integration of the races. ("Lyndon," it was said, "blew with the wind—and sometimes ahead of the wind.") Like many southerners, he did not think it was right that blacks be barred from a voting booth. "If a black man or woman can be asked to fight for his or her country," many southerners said, "they've got the right to vote."

Lyndon went on TV to speak to Congress and the nation after the Selma beatings. This speech would be one of the two most memorable Johnson speeches.

"What happened in Selma," he said, "is part of a larger movement which reaches into every section and state of America.... Their [the blacks'] cause must be our cause too...."

Then, staring directly into the cameras, the familiar, thin, almost menacing smile on his face, this southern white man drawled out the words, slowly and emphatically, of southern blacks:

"And we shall overcome!"

Congressmen rose, roaring. Across the nation blacks and whites wept.

Congress swiftly passed a voting-rights law. The poll tax was dead. Within a few years the South would see what was thought an impossibility before Lyndon Johnson. Black men and women in the South were elected judges, sheriffs, congressmen, city mayors, and state governors.

On the ranch, Lyndon often wore Stetson and boots and chatted with ranch hands about his cattle and horses. More and more, by 1964, his "heart's home," as Lady Bird called the ranch, was the place he most wanted to be.

18

"I'm Sure I'd Go Batty!"

In 1965 Lyndon asked Congress for 115 laws for his Great Society. Ninety of them were passed. One created Medicare. No longer would older people have to worry about staggering hospital and medical bills that could wipe out a life's savings. When Medicare passed, Lyndon said, "Today is a great day for America."

"Kennedy inspired," one aide of Lyndon's said, "which Johnson was not capable of doing, and Johnson delivered."

Most Americans had come to be charmed by Lyndon's folksy Texas ways. They laughed, delighted, when he pulled up a shirt to let newspaper photographers take pictures of the scar left after an operation to remove his gallbladder. (Lady Bird only sighed—what could she do with that man?) Dog lovers protested, but most Americans were amused when Lyndon was photographed holding up his beagles by their ears. He claimed that lifting beagles by the ears did not hurt them, but the beagles, of course, did not get equal time to reply.

Americans, fretting over electric bills, applauded when they read how Lyndon went around at night snapping off White House lights. And they laughed at his down-home Texas humor. Once, speaking of a congressman he thought

Lyndon signs one of the most important laws that he wanted for his Great Society—the Medicare bill. Watching, and clocking the time of the historic signature on July 30, 1965, are Vice President Humphrey and former president Harry Truman. Lyndon went to Truman's home in Independence, Missouri, to sign the bill that Truman had pleaded for as president. Behind Lyndon is Lady Bird, and behind Truman is his wife, Bess.

Relaxing at the White House with visitors, Lyndon picked up his beagle, Her, by the ears. Another beagle watches, wondering if it will be next to get this version of the Johnson Treatment. Dog lovers argued for months about whether or not one could lift a dog by the ears without hurting it. Lyndon argued that the dog felt no pain.

none too bright, Lyndon said, "Gerry can't walk and chew gum at the same time." (Gerry was Congressman Gerald Ford, later president of the United States.)

Walking one day toward a bunch of military helicopters, Lyndon was told by an aide, "That's your helicopter over there, sir."

The commander-in-chief turned slowly and said, "Son, they're *all* my helicopters."

To men and women who served him loyally and, at times, slavishly, he was forever loyal. Bill Deason, his first White Star candidate, held a string of government jobs. In 1965 he was appointed to the Interstate Commerce Commission. Lyndon's high-school orator Gene Latimer still worked for him.

But he could not forgive what he thought was disloyalty. A former Texas newspaperman, Bill Moyers, wrote some of Lyndon's speeches. "Moyers," a Washington reporter wrote in 1966, "was closer to Lyndon than anyone except Lady Bird." The two were almost like father and son. Moyers resigned from the White House staff to take a high-paying job. One day he was photographed having lunch with Bobby Kennedy, who was by then a New York senator. Lyndon saw the photo and shouted that Moyers had been "on the Kennedy payroll for years." He never spoke to Moyers again.

He could tongue-lash his staff so viciously that men in their fifties burst from his office with tears streaming down their leathery faces. "I will never tell anyone," one man told Robert Caro, what Lyndon had yelled at him. One said, "He knew cuss words I had never heard of." Another said, "He made 'em up as he went along."

Yet, minutes after a scolding, he might throw an arm around a man's shoulders and praise him for some long-ago service. People close to Lyndon feared and respected him, but few said they understood him.

Lynda Johnson, tall and statuesque at five feet nine, had graduated from the University of Texas. Luci, a bouncy five feet four, said laughingly that she was "the only blue-eyed child in a brown-eyed family." Both had the dark hair of their parents. Both were idolized by teenage girls, especially Lynda, who was dating handsome movie actor George Hamilton.

The two received hundreds of letters each week. Many asked what it was like to have a Secret Service man follow them all day and even on dates at night. "I can imagine how you feel on dates," wrote a Philadelphia girl. "I'm sure I'd go batty!" But another girl had an idea: "I would go out with the Secret Service agent."

Lynda and Luci bobbed their way through the latest dances, like the frug and the Watusi, at White House

Relaxing at the ranch, Lyndon poses with the statuesque Lynda Bird. Her dark beauty had attracted movie star George Hamilton. Gossip magazines gushed that there might be a wedding in the White House. There were weddings in the White House, but Lynda married Charles Robb and Luci married Patrick Nugent. Luci's marriage ended in divorce. She later remarried. Lynda became the First Lady of Virginia.

parties with their friends. Lynda was once asked, "Are you the one who does the Watusi?" As quick-thinking as any politician, she said, "No, but I'm famous for other things — I'm an American and I'm a Democrat."

At one party, as some sixty girls and boys danced, the president of the United States suddenly walked among them. He smiled and told the guests that college had been good for his daughters. "It has made them more like their mother," he said with a fond smile.

Lyndon's own mother had died in 1958. She had been buried next to her husband on the LBJ ranch.

The ranch. Sunsets on the Perdinales. More and more Lyndon would ask Bird during the next few years of agony, "Should we go back to our heart's home?"

19

"Lyndon Must Go!"

"Hey, hey, L.B.J.,
How many kids did you kill today?
Hey, hey, L.B.J.,
How many kids did you kill today?
Hey, hey ... "

The chant floated through the windows of the White House. It came from a crowd of college students on Pennsylvania Avenue. Those chants were being heard in 1967 across the United States. More and more Americans demanded that the U.S. get out of what they called the "Vietnam bloodbath."

Lyndon stared out from the White House, disgust on his face as he heard the chanting. Many of the college men had long stringy hair and were bearded; the women walked shoeless on dirty feet. "The young people that my daughters bring around," he told an aide, "are not like that. I just can't believe it."

He had trouble believing that many Americans—he called them "turncoats"—thought their country should desert Vietnam. In 1964 the navy had reported that North Vietnamese boats fired torpedoes at a U.S. ship in the Gulf of Tonkin, just off the Vietnamese coast. Angry congressmen told Lyndon that the navy should have blown the Viet-

Visiting Vietnam, Lyndon reviews troops on a rain-swept field. He made two visits to Vietnam to see for himself—as he did in the Pacific during World War II—how Americans were fighting and what more his generals needed.

namese boats out of the water. At Lyndon's suggestion, Congress passed a resolution ordering the commander-in-chief to "take all necessary measures to repel any armed attack" by the North Vietnamese.

The Gulf of Tonkin Resolution, as it was called, passed in the Senate by a vote of 98–2, and in the House by 416–0. It gave Lyndon an overwhelming vote from Congress to throw all of America's military weight against Ho Chi Minh's peasant army.

Waves of bombers swept over Vietnam to blast Ho's hideouts. Battleships thundered off the shore. By 1967 Lyndon had sent more than 250,000 troops to blast Ho's troops back into North Vietnam. But Ho's guerrillas faded like phantoms into the jungles when American bombs fell and American guns roared. Then, stealthily, often at night, the guerrillas crept back to ambush the Americans, planting lethal mines or catching them in murderous crossfire.

By 1967 thousands of American soldiers had been killed, wounded, blinded, and maimed. The casualty lists stretched longer month by month.

Many senators, such as South Dakota's George Mc-Govern, Minnesota's Eugene McCarthy, and New York's Bobby Kennedy, now rose to protest this undeclared war. "We seem bent upon saving the Vietnamese," McGovern told cheering antiwar protestors, "even if we have to kill the Vietnamese people and demolish their country to do it.... I do not intend to remain silent in the face of what I regard as a policy of madness...."

Eighteen-year-olds refused to register for the military draft. They were hauled to jail. Others fled to Canada and Europe. A mood of rebellion swept over college campuses. Older people joined students in antiwar marches. Lyndon knew the country was being torn apart by those against the war and those who said we had to stay until we won.

Billions of dollars were being spent to pay for the war. (Lyndon's dam-building friend, Herman Brown, got more than a billion dollars to build bases in Vietnam.) Lyndon insisted that the Treasury had enough money to pay for his Great Society *and* the war in Vietnam—"guns and butter," as some people put it. There was also enough money, he said, to send Americans flying toward the moon. And in 1966 an American crew took off from the U.S. space launching pad at Cape Kennedy in Florida and landed its craft on the moon. True to the promise of Kennedy, the American space program, first directed by Lyndon, had reached the moon in the sixties.

But taxes rose. Prices soared for food, clothes, and almost everything else. Americans grumbled about "L.B.J.'s war." By 1968 those who thought he was doing a good job had dropped from 55 percent of the population to less than 40 percent.

A general tells an anxious, worried Lyndon the latest news of bloody battles in Vietnam. Looking just as concerned as the president is Vice President Humphrey. By 1967 the fifty-nine-year-old president's receding hair had noticeably grayed.

Other presidents—such as Truman, Eisenhower, and Kennedy—had been officers during combat. They had sent men into battle and knew that some would die.

Lyndon had risked his life in war—but not the lives of others. In the evenings Luci watched him as he frowned in front of the evening TV news. He saw the bodies of Americans, wrapped in bags, hoisted into helicopters. While the commander-in-chief watched, Luci said, he looked like someone "who had a knife thrust into the pit of his stomach and turned over and over. He just physically looked like he was in agony."

One night she watched him read reports about men butchered in battle. He did not look at her or even notice that she was there. "You could see tears coming to his eyes and subsiding and coming and subsiding," she said. His quiet and withdrawn mood, she said, "was a very painful sight for a man who loved company, needed, wanted, and thrived off people so much."

Luci was the most religious of the Johnsons. Once she suggested to her father that they pray for peace. Together, in the quiet White House, they prayed.

Lyndon tried prayer. And he tried to extend a hand toward Ho Chi Minh by ceasing the bombings of North Vietnam. He tried to lure Ho to the peace table with one billion dollars to turn North Vietnam into "a promised land." But unlike congressmen, Ho did not grab at L.B.J. favors. The war roared on, and the list of American dead, wounded, captured, and missing grew toward 50,000.

Antiwar protestors rallied around the husky, tall, and witty Eugene McCarthy. His supporters chanted, "Lyndon must go! Lyndon must go!" In a vote in New Hampshire for delegates to the 1968 Democratic convention, McCarthy startled the nation—and Lyndon—by getting 42 percent of the vote.

Another candidate raced around the country, speaking against the war—Senator Bobby Kennedy. However, Lyndon knew that he, as president, would go to the convention in the summer of 1968 with enough delegates to be renominated.

Lyndon "wanted to stand up and fight those guys out there in Vietnam," an aide said. "And he wanted to fight those guys in the United States who didn't want to fight out there in Vietnam." He wanted to go on building his Great Society, in which there would be no ignorance, prejudice, or poverty.

But he also knew that America could not fight a war while its young people were trying to drag down its leader. "He was getting depressed," an aide said, "by the possibility that the country would become too wearied" to stay with him until victory or peace was won in Vietnam.

And then there was his family. Luci had married a sales executive, Patrick Nugent. They had a baby boy, Patrick Lyndon. The new grandfather nicknamed the baby Lyn.

He talked with a glint in his eyes of walking the Hill Country with his grandchild as he had toddled on those slopes as a child.

Late in 1967 he told Lady Bird, "I've decided that I won't run for reelection." For a speech to Congress early in 1968, he wrote a last paragraph saying that he would not run—but never delivered the paragraph. He said he had forgotten. A press aide, George Christian, chuckled and said, "In his entire life, I doubt that Lyndon Johnson ever forgot anything that he wanted to remember."

For months he hesitated: Should he run or shouldn't he? On a Sunday night, March 31, he decided to speak to the nation on TV. He would announce a new halt in the bombing of North Vietnam. This would be the second speech by Lyndon that Americans who heard it would always remember.

That morning, Lady Bird looked at her husband of more than thirty years. "His face," she said, "was sagging and there was such pain in his eyes as I had not seen since his mother died."

He told Hubert Humphrey that he had made his decision. Late that day he told a speech writer, "There's nobody on my side. Hubert, Luci, they all say I'm wrong."

At 9:00 P.M. that night he sat in front of a desk in the White House as TV cameras pointed at him. "Tonight," he told millions, "I want to talk to you of peace in Vietnam.... "

Viewers stared, bored, as Lyndon announced that there would be another halt in the bombing, the fourteenth of the past few years. He went over all the usual reasons why Ho should sit down for peace talks.

Then, at about 9:35, a smile began to play about his mouth. He was someone relishing a surprise about to be sprung.

A few feet away from the view of the cameras, his daughters sobbed. Lady Bird had a fixed smile on her face.

America could not be divided, he said, especially during this election year, as he sought peace.

The most powerful man in the free world is often the loneliest as he debates with himself about the decisions that he alone can make.

Lyndon's smile grew wider, but his eyes seemed to be wet behind his spectacles.

"Accordingly," he said, "I shall not seek and I will not accept the nomination of my party for another term as your president."

Across the nation people were staring at one another, mouths open. Never had a president left the Oval Office with such an abrupt announcement.

"Thank you for listening," Lyndon said. "Good night and God bless you."

His hands trembled. The cameras' red lights flicked off. Lady Bird walked over to her husband and said, "Nobly done, darling."

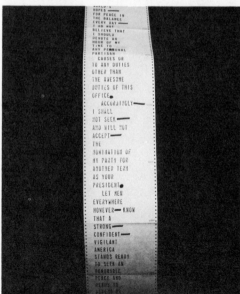

Lyndon speaks to the nation on television on the night of March 31, 1968. That familiar Johnson half smile crept across his face as he said the words, shown here on a Teleprompter tape, to startled Americans: "I shall not seek . . . "

113

20

The Dreamer and the Schemer

Bands blared, flags flapped in the winter wind, crowds cheered. Thousands were massed in front of the Capitol to see the thirty-seventh president of the United States, Richard Nixon, sworn into office. Sitting in the stands on this January morning in 1969 was a smiling Lyndon.

The jut-jawed Nixon shook hands with Lyndon and said, "How do you feel when you aren't president anymore?"

"I don't know whether you'll understand this or not," Lyndon replied, "but you certainly will later. I sat there on the platform and waited for you to stand up and raise your right hand and take the oath of office, and I think that the most pleasant words that . . . ever came into my ears were 'So help me God' that you repeated after that oath."

No longer, Lyndon told Nixon, would he have the fear of being "the man who could make the mistake of involving the world in war."

Nixon had won by defeating Hubert Humphrey for the presidency. Hubert had been nominated by the Democrats after Bobby Kennedy, campaigning for delegates in California, was murdered by Sirhan Sirhan, a crazed immigrant. The Kennedy that Lyndon had disliked so

In retirement, Lyndon went back to his college classrooms at Southwest Texas State Teachers College in San Marcos for a visit and a short talk with students. One of his favorite professors at San Marcos, H. M. Greene, had taught him that "democracy is of necessity a compromise" in which two opposing sides have to come together and agree on a third side — a compromise. Lyndon passed that lesson on to 1970 students at San Marcos.

intensely was suddenly gone. "Johnson was terribly agitated," an aide said, and added, "He must have been filled with a hundred competing emotions."

Lyndon left Washington after Nixon's inauguration and flew back to the ranch. He was a few months past his sixtieth birthday, young for an ex-president. "But he always had a fear he would die in his sixties suddenly, of a heart attack," an aide said — the way his father had died.

He seemed anxious to erect a monument to himself as quickly as possible, one that would tell future Americans what he had done. All his official papers, dating back to his first days in Congress, were brought to Austin from Washington. His rich friends gave money to build a sprawling Lyndon Baines Johnson Library. In May 1971, President Nixon came to dedicate the five-story library. Friend or foe, said Lyndon, could come to the library in Austin to "read and judge," because everything he had done, he said, including his mistakes, was here.

As a president and political campaigner, Lyndon had always liked to "press the flesh," as he put it, shaking hands with voters. Even on foreign trips as the vice president, he rushed into crowds while Secret Service agents stared with horror. Now, in retirement, he greets a horde of delighted and fascinated college students.

The Vietnam War ended in disaster. Americans fled Saigon, the South Vietnamese capital, minutes before the arrival of Ho Chi Minh's troops. Many Americans said Lyndon lost that war and his war against poverty. President Nixon said money was being wasted, and he reduced the money going to antipoverty programs, such as the Jobs Corps. But Medicare and Head Start, two of Lyndon's programs, became as much a part of America as social security. Lyndon's civil-rights laws helped hundreds of blacks to become congressmen, mayors, and governors. "When, one day, there is a black president," a civil-rights leader said, "he can thank Lyndon."

Lyndon roamed the ranch almost every day, inspecting his cattle, riding his horses, chatting with the ranch hands. Often he drove to the farmhouse near the Perdinales where he had been born that stormy night in 1908. It was now a National Park Service tourist attraction. Visitors were often startled to see the tall ex-president, wearing a cowboy hat, stomp into the house, pointing and shouting, "That was my crib!" He had written a book, *The Vantage Point.* He'd point to a stack of his books and yell, "Aren't you gonna buy one?" When visitors did, he sat down and signed copies.

His two daughters, with their children, came to visit. Lynda Bird had married Charles Robb, a lawyer who would, a decade later, become the governor of Virginia. They came bearing the gifts he loved to get. All his life he had relished getting presents—not practical things, like socks, but flashy things, like a belt with a gold buckle. And he was always handing out presents to people as they left, more often than not a small bust of himself.

During the last few months of 1972, his visitors noticed that his face was often ash-gray, his step slower. Talking to someone, he winced, pain stabbing at his chest. Doc-

At the opening of the LBJ Library in Austin in 1971, President Nixon and Lyndon, two old foes from their Senate days, tour the grounds together. Hurrying to catch up are Pat Nixon and Lady Bird.

117

tors said he had angina, a heart disease. Lady Bird tried to stop him when he wanted to do too much.

One day a busload of schoolchildren from a poor neighborhood in Austin were killed in a highway accident. Lyndon insisted on going to the funeral. "These people are my people," he told Lady Bird. "When nobody else was with me, they stood by me." He went to the funeral.

He was resting alone in his bedroom on the afternoon of January 22, 1973. He called a switchboard operator and asked that a Secret Service agent come to him quickly.

Two came running. They saw Lyndon lying on the floor next to the bed.

Lady Bird was in Austin. She was told that Lyndon was being flown to a San Antonio hospital. When she got there, a doctor told her that he was dead.

Lyndon's body was buried next to his parents on the ranch. During the burial ceremony, an old black man

A retired, relaxed President scoots around the ranch in a cart. His passengers are a family dog, Luci and her son Patrick Lyndon, Lyn to his granddaddy.

On January 25, 1973, the coffin carrying the thirty-sixth president of the United States is taken to its final resting place on the LBJ Ranch. Lady Bird and her daughters are at the left. In the background to the right are John Connally and his wife, Nellie. On the right are the graves of Lyndon's mother and father.

hobbled up to Luci and said, "Ma'am, you don't have to tell me he loved me. He *showed* me he loved me."

L.B.J. No American of the last half century stood so long so close to power. As a young congressman, he whispered into the ear of a president. As a senator he stood with a Speaker and a president as one of the three most powerful political leaders in the country. As a vice president for three years, he sat next to the free world's most powerful man. As a president for five years, he was the free world's most powerful person.

He needed power. "It has a smell," he once said. He needed to be feared, respected, even adored. No jealous farmhand would ever again knock him down and humiliate him. By guile or by the force of his stinging tongue-

Near the end of his life, Lyndon—a Texan at heart and in style—looks out at the Hill Country that he loved.

lashings, he stomped over or swept around anyone who stood in the way of his reaching his goal of being a "somebody."

He was a Johnson and a Bunton, a dreamer and a schemer. The dreamer was loved, the schemer despised. But without the scheming, many of the dreams—civil-rights laws and Medicare among them—might have stayed only dreams. Great dreamers and great schemers often make great presidents.

Was Lyndon a great president?

Historians will argue the question for decades. This much can be said with certainty: There was never, *never* any president like him.

Index

NEW YORK MILLS
PUBLIC LIBRARY

401 Main Street
New York Mills, N.Y. 13417

(315) 736-5391

MEMBER

MID-YORK LIBRARY SYSTEM
Utica, N.Y. 13502